I0120353

King of England Edward VI, Robert Potts

King Edward the Sixth on the supremacy

The French original and an English translation. With his discourse on the

reformation of abuses ; and a few brief notices of his life, education, and death

King of England Edward VI, Robert Potts

King Edward the Sixth on the supremacy
The French original and an English translation. With his discourse on the
reformation of abuses ; and a few brief notices of his life, education, and death

ISBN/EAN: 9783741155475

Manufactured in Europe, USA, Canada, Australia, Japa

Cover: Foto ©Andreas Hilbeck / pixelio.de

Manufactured and distributed by brebook publishing software
(www.brebook.com)

King of England Edward VI, Robert Potts

King Edward the Sixth on the supremacy

KING EDWARD THE SIXTH

ON

THE SUPREMACY.

The French Original and an English Translation.

WITH HIS DISCOURSE ON THE REFORMATION OF ABUSES;
AND A FEW BRIEF NOTICES OF HIS LIFE, EDUCATION, AND DEATH.

EDITED BY

ROBERT POTTS, M.A. TRIN. COLL. CAMBRIDGE;

HON. LL.D:, WILLIAM AND MARY COLLEGE, VA.

CAMBRIDGE:
PUBLISHED BY WILLIAM METCALFE, TRINITY STREET.
LONDON:
SOLD AT THE NATIONAL SOCIETY'S DEPOSITORY, WESTMINSTER.
———
1874.

CONTENTS.

INTRODUCTION.

The short Treatise of King Edward the Sixth on the Supremacy is a literary curiosity, whether it be regarded in reference to its author or its subject.

Since the publication of the Vatican Decree, the subject has assumed a high degree of importance, and at the present time it engages the serious attention of some of the Governments of Europe. The supremacy usurped, and attempted to be exercised over all Christian peoples and nations, is of such a nature as to be utterly subversive of all National Governments which are not subject or subservient to the infallible Pontiff of Rome. From the recent action taken in Switzerland and Germany against the agents of Rome in attempts made to enforce the Syllabus on their subjects, it may be fairly inferred that the Vatican Decree is regarded as a conspiracy against the sovereign powers of these States. It may be found desirable, if not necessary, at no distant day, for the nations of Europe to agree to some international laws for the mutual defence of their Governments against this supreme "Regiment of Priests," as these nations

have already agreed to act in concert for the abolition
of the slavery of the human race.

With reference to the Royal author. He composed
this little treatise *before he was fourteen years of age, in
the French language.* The work exhibits an extent of
knowledge and a measure of intellectual cultivation
far beyond what might have been expected at so
early an age, and it may fairly be taken to represent
the views and opinions held at that time on the subject. Some years had now passed since his father
with the aid of his Parliament had confirmed the law
of supremacy, by the Act for the Extinguishment of
the authority of the Bishop of Rome. The youthful
son of King Henry VIII. appears to have fully appre-
hended the importance of the Royal Supremacy, in
carrying out, without external interference, the Reformation, both Civil and Religious, and .his short life
affords ample evidence of his sincerity. The young
King dedicated the little treatise to his uncle, the
Duke of Somerset, the Lord Protector of his Royal
person.

The present publication is an attempt to exhibit
the Short. Treatise of King Edward the Sixth in
the same form, page for page, line for line, and
word for word, as the original copy exists in his own
handwriting.

This original is still preserved in the University
Library of Cambridge (Dd. xii. 59), having been pre-
sented by Edward Cannon, M.A., Fellow of King's
College, Cambridge. It is a small book in boards with

a calf leather back. According to Nasmith, it was originally bound in green velvet with gilt edges, which are still dimly visible. It is written on paper; the leaves are in length and breadth about 6·5 and 4·5 inches respectively. The manuscript contains a hundred pages, but the number of lines on each page is not always the same. The same number of lines, however, on each page of the manuscript, has been strictly retained in the printed impression.

The sizes of type employed nearly correspond to the size of the letters in the manuscript, which are in form nearer the ordinary Roman letters than the manuscript writing of that age. The variations in spelling the same words have been retained, and the same division of words, not by syllables, as at present, but variously by letters, has been rigidly adhered to in every respect. Instead of retaining the few abbreviations, it was deemed better to print the omitted letter or letters, where any abbreviations occur.

In the British Museum (MSS. Addit. 5464) is preserved among the manuscripts of King Edward VI. a copy of an Essay, of which the first page is headed, "Alencontre les abus du Monde, 13 De. 1548," and the last page is dated in the same handwriting "14 Mars, 1549." It would appear from this title that the King had first proposed to himself to write on this subject, but afterwards changed his intention to write on that of "Alencontre de la Primauté du Pape." To Mr. Nicholls* belongs the credit of the

* "Notes and Queries," Second Series, vol. i. pp. 112, 113 : 1856.

discovery that this essay is really the original rough draft of the King's Short Treatise against the Pope's Supremacy. The copy of this draft is in King Edward's handwriting, corrected throughout by the hand of his French master, Mons. Belmaine; and the copy preserved in the University Library at Cambridge is the fair transcript made by the King himself for presentation to his uncle, the Duke of Somerset. At the end of the manuscript copy in the British Museum is the following testimony, apparently written by the King's French master :—

"Tout ainsi qu'un bon Paintre peut répresenter le visage, regard, contenance et corpulence d'un Prince: Ainsi par les escritz, parolles et actions d'un Prince ou peut facilement entendre quel esprit est en luy, et aquoy Il est adonné, comme on peut veoir par les Escritz de ce jeune Roy, Lequel composa et escrivit ce Livre, n'ayant encores douze ans accomplis, et sans l'ayde de parsonne vivant, excepté des propos qu'il avoit ouys de plusieurs, et la souvenance qu'il avoit des livres qu'il avoit leuz. Car dès ce qu'il commenca a escrivre ledict livre, et jusques a ce qu'il l'eust achevé, ledict livre a tousjours esté en ma garde jusques a présent."

The English translation of King Edward's Short Treatise, which follows the original French in this volume, is a copy of the translation published in London in the year 1682. A copy of the book is preserved in the University Library at Cambridge (7, 39, 90). It bears the following title-page, "The

Pope's Supremacy confuted by King Edward the VI.
Translated out of his French original."

Under this title are printed—

Luke ii. 42.—And when he was twelve years old, they went up to
Jerusalem, &c.

Ver. 46.—And it came to pass, that after three days they found him
in the Temple, sitting in the midst of the Doctors.

Ver. 47.—And all that heard him were astonished at his understanding and answers.

and beneath, "London: printed by J. D., for Jonathan
Robinson, at the Golden Lion in St. Paul's Church-
Yard, 1682." In the address of the publisher to the
reader is stated—"The Prince's autographon of the
treatise against the Papacy now published, was
found in the French tongue, in the Library of one
of the most eminently learned men of the last age,
and is here presented, as it was faithfully translated by
a person of very high quality in this." There are
no traces in the publisher's remarks which enable the
reader to discover the name of this distinguished per-
sonage. That he was a man of high honour may be
inferred from his calm vindication of King Edward's
memory from the unjust and sneering censures of
Dr. Heylin.

This translation, with some slight alterations, was
reprinted in the year 1810, with the following title:—

"A Declaration against the Pope's Supremacy; by
his Majesty Edward the Sixth, King of Great Britain,
France, and Ireland, Defender of the Faith; Dedicated
to his uncle, the Duke of Somerset, Protector of his
person, and Regent of his Kingdom, in the year 1549.

Now republished and dedicated to His Majesty George
the Third, by the Rev. John Duncan, LL.D., F.A.S.

" Blessed art thou, O Lord, when thy king is the son of nobles, and
thy princes eat in due season."—*Solomon*.

Chelsea: Printed by J. Tilling, and sold by Hatchard,
Piccadilly, etc. 1810."

A copy of Dr. Duncan's reprint is not found in the
University Library at Cambridge, nor in the Library
of the British Museum. The book is not often met
with. There is a copy of the book in the Library of
the Protestant Educational Institute in London. Tho
following dedication is prefixed by Dr. Duncan to his
reprint of the translation.

" To the King.

"Sire, I have recently come in possession of a royal
jewel of considerable value ; it descends from one of
your royal predecessors. I therefore presume to revive
and present it for your Majesty's acceptance : I con-
ceive no one else has such a natural right to it as your
Majesty. I have been induced to do so at this time,
as the subject-matter of it is coming before both your
Majesty's honourable Houses of Lords and Commons.

" One of your Majesty's sacred titles is concerned in
the following pages ; your coronation engagement is
still solemn, and binding, as at first; hitherto your
Majesty has faithfully fulfilled it, which has endeared
you to your subjects beyond any of your predecessors.

" All ranks and professions among us highly esteem
your Majesty and Government. We thank Almighty

God for prolonging your life to such a period, as to be
the father of all the reigning monarchs in Europe;
and, if consistent with the Divine will, we earnestly
pray, that your valuable life may yet be lengthened
many years for the comfort of your family, and happiness of your kingdoms—that God may keep your
Majesty, faithful to your sacred trust in matters of
religion, laws, and liberty—that you may leave them
pure and undiminished to your royal successor; and
when you shall have finished your generation work
among your people on earth, may you be blessed with
a happy demise, to reign with the King of kings in
glory to all eternity, which is the sincere prayer of
                    "Sire,
            "Your Majesty's faithful subject
                and devoted servant,
"Palace Street,   "John Duncan.
    "Buckingham Gate,
        "May, 1810."

To the Short Treatise on the Supremacy has been
added the young King's discourse on the Reformation
of Abuses. As the literary composition of a youth, it
contains many wise suggestions, some of them not
unsuitable for the present time, and forms one of the
most important of the pieces that remain in the King's
handwriting. It appears to have been suggested by
the written advice of M. Bucer. It is to be re-
gretted that what remains of this discourse is only
a fragment, and it may be doubted if the discourse
itself was ever completed by the King.

Tho Literary Remains of King Edward the Sixth have been edited with Historical Notes, and a Biographical Memoir, by John Gough Nicholls, Esq., F.S.A., and printed in two quarto volumes, for the Roxburgh Club. In Mr. Nicholls's volumes (printed in 1859) the reader will find almost every matter of interest connected with the life and writings of King Edward VI.

A FEW BRIEF NOTICES OF THE LIFE, EDUCATION, AND DEATH OF KING EDWARD THE SIXTH.

The following brief notices of the youthful King, and the testimonies of his contemporaries to his mental and moral qualities, his docility, love of learning, and earnestness in matters of religion, may not be uninteresting to the reader.

King Henry VIII., the Founder of Trinity College, Cambridge, was a great patron of learning,* and was

---

* The following two anecdotes illustrate the King's opinion of learning and ignorance :—

"Whilst at Abingdon he [Sir Thomas More] was called upon, also, to interfere with his influence to quiet a foolish excitement which had seized the students at Oxford. It was not the spread of the sweating sickness which had caused them alarm ; but the increasing taste for the study of Greek had roused the fears of divines of the old school. The enemies of the 'new learning' had raised a faction against it. The students had taken sides, calling themselves Greeks and Trojans, and not content with wordy warfare, they had come to open and public insult. At length the most virulent abuse had been poured upon the Greek language and literature, even from the University pulpit, by an impudent and ignorant preacher. He had denounced all who favoured Greek studies as ' heretics ;' in his coarse phraseology, those who taught the obnoxious language were ' *diabolos maximos*,' and the students ' *diabolos minutulos*.'

careful to select the ablest and the best instructors for
his children. His son Prince Edward was born on
12th October, 1537, and in his journal he has recorded
that he was brought up "among the women" until he
was six years of age. After this time, he does not

More, upon hearing what had been passing, wrote a letter of indig-
nant but respectful remonstrance to the University authorities. He
and Pace interested the King also in the affair, and at their suggestion
he took occasion to express his royal pleasure that the students 'would
do well to devote themselves with energy and spirit to the study of
Greek literature ;' 'and so,' says Erasmus, 'silence was imposed upon
these brawlers.'

"On another occasion the King and his courtiers had attended Divine
service. The court preacher had, like the Oxford divine, indulged in
abuse of Greek literature and the modern school of interpretation,
having Erasmus and his New Testament in his eye. Pace looked at
the King to see what he thought of it. The King answered his look
with a satirical smile. After the sermon the divine was ordered to
attend upon the King. It was arranged that More should reply to the
arguments he had urged against Greek literature. After he had done
so, the divine, instead of replying to his arguments, dropped down
upon his knees before the King, and simply prayed for forgiveness,
urging, however, by way of extenuating his fault, that he was carried
away by the spirit in his sermon when he poured forth all his abuse
of the Greek language. 'But,' the King here observed, 'that spirit
was not the spirit of *Christ*, but the spirit of *foolishness*.' He then
asked the preacher what works of Erasmus he had read. He had not
read any. 'Then,' said the King, 'you prove yourself to be a fool, for
you condemn what you have never read.' 'I read once,' replied the
divine, 'a thing called the "Moria."' . . . Pace here suggested that
there was a decided congruity between that and the preacher. And
finally the preacher himself relented so far as to admit :—'After all I am
not so *very* hostile to Greek letters, because they are derived from the
Hebrew.' The King, wondering at the distinguished folly of the man,
bade him retire, but with strict injunctions never again to preach at
court."—*The Oxford Reformers, Colet, Erasmus, and More, by Frederic
Seebohm, 2nd ed. 1869, pp. 458—460.*

appear to have had much of the society of his sisters,
the Princess Mary and the Princess Elizabeth; as
both of them had their own separate households.
It was the custom of those times to associate four
or more children of good disposition and generous
manners to be educated with the King's son, so that
by their good example he might be induced to profit
in his learning. Several noble associates were brought
up with Prince Edward when he was placed under
the care of preceptors. And it is not improbable
that Cranmer, the prince's godfather, was consulted in
the selection of them. The first preceptor chosen for
the young prince was Dr. Richard Coxe. He had been
Master of Eton, and was a man of strict integrity,
amiable manners, and of great experience in teaching.
Mr. (afterwards Sir) John Cheke in 1544 was appointed
" as a supplement to Dr. Coxe," both for the better
instruction of the prince, and the diligent teaching of
such children as might be appointed to attend upon
him. The prince in his journal has stated that his two
preceptors Dr. Coxe and Mr. Cheke instructed him " in
the learning of tongues, of the Scriptures, of philosophy,
and all liberal sciences." He also adds that John Belmaine, a Frenchman, taught him the French language.
The prince was instructed in the art of writing by
Roger Ascham, who, on account of his exquisite hand,
had been also appointed to teach his younger sister, the
Princess Elizabeth. Sir Anthony Cooke, famous for
his five learned daughters, was another of Prince
Edward's preceptors. It is not certain when he was

appointed, but his appointment was probably made on the retirement of Dr. Coxe from that office. The direction, however, of the education of Prince Edward appears to have devolved chiefly on Mr. Cheke, on whose appointment, Roger Ascham makes the following remarks :—

"Our noble King, full of wysedome, hath called up this excellent man, ful of learnynge, to teache noble Prince Edwarde, an office ful of hope, comforte, and solace to al true hertes of England; for whome al England dayly doth praye, that he, 'passing his tutour in learnyng and knowledge, folowynge his father in wisedome and felicitie, accordyng to that example which is set afore his eyes, may so set out and mayntayne Goddes worde, to the abolishment of al papistry, the confusion of al heresie, that therby he, feared of his ennemies, loved of al his subjectes, may bring to his own glory immortal fame and memorie; to this realme, welthe, honour, and felicitie; to true and unfayned religion, perpetual peace, concorde and unitie."*

An extract from a letter of Dr. Coxe, written in 1545, gives the following account of the character and acquirements of his pupil :—

"He hath expugned and utterly conquered a great number of the captains of Ignorance. The eight parts of speech he hath made them his subjects and servants, and can decline any manner of Latin noun, and conjugate a verb perfectly, unless it be anomalum. These parts, thus beaten down and conquered, he beginneth to

* Toxophilus, Bk. 1, fol. 34, 1545.

build them up again, and frame them after his purpose
with due order of construction. . . . , .

" He understandeth and can frame well his three con-
cords of grammar, and hath made already forty or fifty
pretty Latin verses, and can answer well favouredly to
the parts, and is now ready to enter into Cato, to some
proper and profitable fables of Æsop, and other
wholesome and godly lesson that shall be devised
for him. .

" Every day in the mass time he readeth a portion
of Solomon's Proverbs, for the exercise of his reading,
wherein he delighteth much ; and learneth there how
good it is to give ear unto discipline, to fear God, to
keep God's commandments, to beware of strange and
wanton women, to be obedient to father and mother,
to be thankful to him who telleth him of his faults."

The three following letters of Prince Edward exhibit some indications of his dutiful disposition :—

" Regiæ Majestati,

" Cum tot et tanta in me contuleris beneficia,
Rex nobilissime atque pater pientissime, quæ vix
numerare queam ; tum hæc strena, quam ad me postre-
mum misisti, videtur mihi non solum præclara,
verumetiam paternæ tuæ pietatis erga me ple-
nissima, ob quam ingentes tibi gratias ago ; et cogito
me, quamquam adnitar pro viribus omne tempus
vitæ meæ, et laborem in omni genere officiorum,
tamen vix magnitudinem beneficiorum tuorum at-
tingere posse. Quare conabor, quod natura et officium

me postulant, majestati tuæ placere, atque esse optimi
patris bonus filius, ac sequi exemplum virtutis,
sapientiæ, et pietatis tuæ. Quam rem spero tibi
futuram gratissimam. Atque hoc melius præstabo,
si pergas in benevolentia tua erga me, et mihi
quotidianam tuam benedictionem impertias. Dominus
Jesus te servet incolumem.

"Hartfordiæ, decimo Januarii anno 1546.

"E. Princeps."

To Queen Katharine [translation from Latin].

"Pardon my rude style in writing to you, most
illustrious Queen and beloved Mother, and receive
my hearty thanks for your loving kindness to me
and my sister. Yet, dearest Mother, the only true
consolation is from Heaven, and the only real love
is the love of God. Preserve, therefore, I pray you,
my dear sister Mary from all the wiles and enchant-
ments of the Evil one, and beseech her to attend
no longer to foreign dances and merriments which
do not become a most Christian Princess. And so,
putting my trust in God for you to take this exhortation in good part, I commend you to his most gracious
keeping.

"Edward, the Prince.

"From Hunsdon, this 12th of May [1546]."

To Queen Katharine [Without date].

"Most honorable and entierly beloved mother, I
have me most humbli recommended unto youre grace,

with lyke thankes, both for that your grace ded
accepte so gentylly my simple and rude letters, and
also that it pleased your grace so gentylly to vowch-
saufe to directe unto mo your loving and tendre
letters, which do geve me much comfort and encou-
ragement to go forward in such thinges whorin
your grace bereath. me on hand that I am already
entered.

"I pray God I maie be hable in part to satisfy
the good expectation of the Kinges Majesti my
father and of your grace: whom God have ever
in his most blessed keping.

"Your loving sonne,
"E. Prince."

King Edward VI. was crowned in Westminster
Abbey by Cranmer, the Archbishop of Canterbury,
who, instead of the usual Sermon, delivered a brief
charge,—admonishing the King of his duty, especially
in respect of Religion—from which the following
passage is taken:—

"Therefore not from the bishop of Rome, but as a
messenger from my Saviour Jesus Christ, I shall most
humbly admonish your Royal Majesty, what things
your Highness is to perform.

"Your Majesty is God's vice-gerent and Christ's vicar
within your own dominions, and to see, with your predecessor Josiah, God truly worshipped, and idolatry
destroyed, the tyranny of the bishops of Rome banished
from your subjects, and images removed. These acts
be signs of a second Josiah, who reformed the Church

of God in his days. You are to reward virtue, to revenge sin, to justify the innocent, to relieve the poor, to procure peace, to repress violence, and to execute justice throughout your realms. For precedents, on those kings who performed not these things, the old law shews how the Lord revenged his quarrel; and on those kings who fulfilled these things, he poured forth his blessings in abundance. For example, it is written of Josiah in the book of the Kings thus: 'Like unto him there was no king before him that turned to the Lord with all his heart, according to all the Law of Moses, neither after him were there any like him.' This was to that Prince a perpetual fame of dignity, to remain to the end of his days."

The following anecdote is mentioned by Strype:—
"At the Coronation of King Edward, which was on Shrove-Sunday, Feb. 20, 1547, an author that wrote about these times [Bal. de Viris Illustrib.] relates that he heard it from credible hands, that when three swords were brought, signs of his being king of three kingdoms, he said, there was one yet wanting. And when the nobles about him asked him what that was, he answered, *The Bible.* 'That book,' added he, 'is the sword of the Spirit, and to be preferred before these swords. That ought in all right to govern us, who use them for the people's safety by God's appointment. Without that sword, we are nothing, we can do nothing, we have no power. From that we are what we are this day. From that we receive whatsoever it is that we at this present do assume. He that rules without it, is

not to be called God's minister, or a King. Under that
wo ought to live, to fight, to govern the people, and to
perform all our affairs. From that alone wo obtain ull
power, virtue, graco, salvation, and whatsoever we
have of divine strength.' And when the pious young
king had said this, and some other like words, he commanded the Bible, with tho greatest roverence, to be
brought and carried before him."

The following is a translation of a Latin lotter of
King Edward to Katharine, the Queen Dowager.

" Since I was not far from you, and in hopes every
day to see you, I thought it best to write no letter at
all to you. For letters are tokens of remembrance and
kindness between such as are at a great distance. But
being at length moved by your request, I could not
forbear to send you a letter ; first, to do somewhat that
may be acceptable to you ; and then, to answer your
letter, full of kindness, which you sent me from St.
James's. In which, first, you set before mine eyes your
love toward my father the King, of most noble memory;
then, your good wish towards me : and, lastly, your
godliness, your knowledge and learning in the Scriptures. Go on therefore in your good enterprise, and
continue to love my father, and to shew so great tokens
of kindness to me, which I have hitherto ever perceived
in you. And cease not to love and read the Scriptures :
but hold out always in reading them. For in the first,
you shew the duty of a good wife and a good subject ;
in the second, the praise of your friendship ; and in
the third, your piety towards God.

Wherefore, since you love my father, I cannot but
much commend you; since you love me, I cannot but
love you again : and since you love God's word, I will
love and admire you from my heart. Wherefore, if
there be any thing wherein I may do you a kindness,
I shall do it willingly. Farewell.

"The 30th of May [1547]."

In the year 1547, Mr. (afterwards Sir) John Cheke
had a very dangerous illness, and despairing of recovery,
he wrote the following valedictory letter to his former
pupil, King Edward :—

"Because I am departing, my sovereign lord, unto
the King of all kings, Almighty God, and must by his
appointment leave you, whom of long time I have done
my best to bring up in virtue and good learning ; and
you are now coming to a government of yourself, in
which estate I pray God you may always be served
with them that will faithfully, truly, and plainly give
you counsel. I have thought it my duty, for a memory
of my last will, and for a token of my well-wishing
unto you (remaining presently with me, even as it hath
always heretofore done), to require you, yea, and in
God's behalf to charge you, that, forasmuch as years
both have and will diminish in you the fear of man,
to have yet before your eyes continually the fear of
God ; with the which if you do not direct, order, and
temper all your doings and sayings, be you well as-
sured neither to have good success in the great charge
that he hath committed to you, neither in the end
to enjoy that joyful place that is promised timentibus

eum. For if God do right extremely punish men of base estate, and of low degrees, for wanting of that necessary jewel, which hath in Scripture so many promises: how severely will He punish kings and princes failing therein, in whom the lack thereof must needs be both to themselves and to the commonwealth most perilous.

"My weakness suffereth me, not so long to talk with you in this matter as I could wish, and your Majesty's disposition (which I know most apt to receive all godly admonitions) putteth me in comfort to think this to be sufficient, beseeching God so to direct all your doings, thoughts and meanings, as may tend to his glory and your honour and wealth, both here and in the world to come, when by death you shall be called thereunto; to the which all men, as well princes as others, as well young as old, are subject.

"Most affectionately beseeching your grace, if any of your servants about you shall frankly admonish you of any thing which in you may be misliked, to take it at their hands, and think them that shall so do, to be your only servants of trust; and to consider them, and to reward them accordingly. And if any such shall be, that shall of all things make fair weather, and, whatsoever they shall see to the contrary, shall tell you, *all is well;* beware of them, they serve themselves, and not you.

"And where you have read, in the time that it hath pleased God to lend me unto you, divers discourses of divers sorts, as well of stories, as of philosophy, whereby you have had profit, and plenty of grave and wise rules

and orders for the good government of your realm; yet,
in mine opinion, among them all, none hath so abun-
dantly furnished you in those points as hath Aristotle,
to whom I beseech you, for those matters, often to
resort, and especially to two chapters in his Politics,
the one De Mutatione regni, &c., and the other per
quœ regna servantur, being the tenth and eleventh
chapters of the S. of his Politics.

"For your Divinity, I would wish you would diligently
continue the reading of the New Testament, with
Sapientia, Ecclesiasticus, and the Proverbs.

"And, understanding that it hath pleased you (sithen
the time of my sickness) to send unto me many com-
fortable messages, and among the rest, that you have
appointed (much unto my comfort) the wardship of my
son to his mother; like as I do therefore render unto
your Grace my most humble thanks so to do, I with
like humbleness desire you (my great debts considered)
to remit to him, if all shall be too much, yet some
convenient piece of such lands as, during his nonage,
shall fall unto you.

"And whereas I shall now leave my college in Cambridge destitute of a head, if your Grace appoint thereunto Mr. Haddon, I think you shall appoint a worthy
man.

"Finally, one suit charity moveth me to make
unto your Majesty: the Bishop of Chichester was my
bringer-up, and at his hands I gate an entry to some skill
in learning; living I could never do him any good
whereby I might be accompted a grateful scholar; if

dying I might attain for him liberty, with some small aid of living, I should be much bound unto you, thinking most assuredly you shall find of him, during his life, both a daily beadsman for you, and a right obedient subject; though in some things heretofore, he hath more thoroughly persuaded his conscience, than to the perfection of Christ's religion was requisite.

"Thus the Living God preserve your Majesty long to reign most prosperously. Out of my death bed." *

In the month of April or May, 1549, Sir John Cheke wrote the following letter to the Lord Protector, on the moral education of King Edward :—

"The letters which your Grace sent to the University [of Cambridge] for the better expedition of the visitation, hath encouraged men's studies marvellously to the further desire of learning, and established the doubtful minds of some wavering men, which took all unknown matters to the worst, and feared shadows of mistrusted things, whereof they had no cause. Wherefore, your Grace, in mine opinion, hath done a very beneficial deed to the schools, whose head and chancellor you be, in speeding out of hand this visitation ; and shall make hereby a number of honest and learned men to serve the King's Majesty faithfully in their calling another day, which is one chief point of every subject's duty to labour in: and hereby all sorts of students knowing the King's Majesty toward in hope of all excellency to learning ; and your Grace hold-

* Harrington's Nugæ Antiquæ. Vol. i. pp. 17—22.

ing the stern of honour, not only ordering all matters
of counsel with wisdom, but also considering the further-
ance of learning with favour; be stirred and enabled to
attain to a greater and perfecter trade of learning, not
unbehovable for the commonwealth, nor unserviceable
for the King's Majesty, nor unpleasant to your Grace,
by whose authority it now the better springeth.

"For which cause I suppose among other, the
King's Majesty hath great occasion to give God thanks,
that not only in his minority his realm is governed
at home with your sage, ancient counsel, and de-
fended from the foreign incursion of great and power-
ful adversaries, but also provision is made for learned
men to serve his grace hereafter; whose use shall be
necessary for the realm, not only for religion, but
also for civil causes. And therefore, as I may say
boldly to your Grace, I, often thinking of his Majesty,
trust he will now make him (according to all men's
certain expectation) worthy another day so noble an
uncle; and so toward a number of youth preparing
themselves aforehand to serve his Majesty's commonwealth hereafter; which he cannot do only by greatness of natural wit, whereof he hath sufficient, except
he adjoin also experience (the very ground-work of all
wisdom) wherein his Majesty best shall be advertised
by you. For all learning, be it never so great, except
it be sifted with much use and experience to the finest,
can be no wisdom, but only a void and a waste knowledge; and therefore this kind can be learned by no
book, but only by diligent hearing of sage and ex-

perienced counsellors, and following more their good
advice, who doth foresee the greatness of dangers to
come, unconceived and unthought of by others, than
their own sudden fancies, who, for lack of farther in-
sight, do judge their own counsel best, because they
do perceive in themselves no reason against themselves;
although there be in the thing itself, and wise men's
heads, never so much to the contrary. Wherefore, as
his Majesty hath always learned, so I trust he laboureth
daily to avoid the ground of all error, that self-pleasing,
which the Greeks do call φιλαυτία; when a man delighteth in his own reason, and despiseth other men's
counsel, and thinketh no man's foresight to be so good
as his, nor no man's judgment compared to his own:
for, if there be any wisdom, it is conferring with many
wise heads, and of divers good counsels, to choose out
one perfect, and so to follow that which reasonable
experience leadeth a man witty unto.

"And, if there be any hindrance and stop to wisdom,
it is where fancy favoureth a man's own invention, and
he hath a better opinion of his own reason than it
deserveth indeed, and so alloweth it to be good, and
sticketh to his sense by self-love; or ever he know
what it is worth by proof of reason; and therefore is
not constant therein by judgment, but headstrong by
wilfulness.

"And this thing is to be avoided diligently of all,
and especially of the King's Majesty, now in this
tenderness of his youth; because every fault is greater
in a king than in a mean man, and also faults rooted

in this age do not only grow to a greatness, but also they utterly take away the likelihood of divers good virtues which else would spring freshly in it. I do wish therefore oftentimes, that which the King's Majesty was wont to labour in, that he continued to be an Academic, slow to judge, glad to hear all men, mistrusting his own reason, taking truth to be hidden, and so not to be found at the first sight; thinking wisdom either to be in men of experience, or else in no men ; and always persuading himself in his youth, which Socrates believed when he was old, *that he knoweth this only thing, that yet he knew nothing ;* and so shall he best avoid the bottomless dangers, unknown faults, which will else unawares creep into his mind. Not only in warfare but also in peace, it is dangerous for a public person to say, *Had I known,* to excuse the matter, with a *putari* to maintain on that reason, whose beginning is grounded on an error. The King's Majesty knoweth herein half what I mean, and the sure safeguard of wisdom and happiness is to avoid the first fault, which is first commanded to be avoided in ' Tullie's Offices.'*

"But what mean I to write this to your Grace, especially knowing the King's Majesty's nature, how glad he is to follow your Grace's good advertisements, and willing to obey all those who be put in trust about him. I have no cause to mistrust, but love is full of fear when there is no cause, and my duty ready

* " The taking up of things upon trust, and flattering ourselves that we know more than effectually we do." Lib. I.

to admonish aforehand, for fear of a cause; and yet my hope is, there will be no cause; for I cannot (by nature as a subject, by duty as a servant) but continually wish to his Majesty daily increase of God's marvellous gift well begun in him, and to your Grace much honour for the great burden of unsufferable pains which you sustain in his minority for his cause; not doubting but, as God of his goodness doth prosper all your affairs with good success, so will the King's Majesty, as he is most bounden, thankfully consider and liberally recompense, another day, those your infinite travails in his commonwealth."[*]

The following short extract is taken from a Latin letter of Roger Ascham to Joannes Sturmius, written in the spring of 1550 :—

"The nobility of England was never more devoted to literature than at present. Our most illustrious King Edward, alike in ability, in industry, perseverance, and acquirements, far exceeds what is usually expected from his years. It is from no fond reports, but from my own frequent observation, which I regard as the sweetest incident of my good fortune, that I have contemplated the whole band of virtues taking up their residence in his breast."

In another Latin letter of Roger Ascham, written to Sturmius on 14th December, 1550, are contained the following particulars of the progress of King Edward's education, as communicated by Sir John Cheke :—

"He shall hear from you how honourable it is for a

[*] Harrington's Nugæ Antiquæ. Vol. I. pp. 41—47.

ruler to study wisdom, and how a commonwealth is to be governed by good counsel, not by good luck; whilst the best counsels are to be derived from the best books, and, next to Holy Writ, there are none more suited to frame wise counsel than those of Aristotle; although the King, such is the excellence of his nature, requires no spur to hasten that career of learning and wisdom, into which he has most happily entered.

"Our King's ability equals his fortune, and his goodness surpasses both: or rather, as it becomes a Christian man to speak, such is the manifold grace of God, that in eagerness for the best literature, in pursuit of the most perfect religion, in willingness, in judgment, and in perseverance, that quality you most value in study, he wonderfully exceeds his years. In scarce any other particular do I esteem him more fortunate than that he has obtained John Cheke as the instructor of his youth in sound learning and true religion. Latin he understands with accuracy, speaks with propriety, writes with facility combined with judgment. In Greek he has learned the Dialectic of Aristotle, and now learns his Ethic. He has proceeded so far in that language, that he readily translates the Latin of Cicero's Philosophia into Greek. On the day before I left England, when conversing in London with Sir John Cheke, I inquired of him how it was that the King should read the Ethic of Aristotle rather than the Cyropædia of Xenophon, and he answered with the greatest wisdom and learning, (as he is always wont,) 'in order that his mind, first instructed in all those infinite examinations and dissections of the virtues and vices, may bring a sound judgment to each of those examples of character and conduct that everywhere present themselves in history: and because it is scarcely possible that his natural perceptions, amused and led away by the pleasantness of history, should at once form such conclusions as are of an abstruse and recondite nature, although highly necessary to confirm the judgment. Still my endeavour is to give him no precept unaccompanied by some remarkable example.' How fortunate (adds Ascham) is England, my Sturmius, that the youth of its prince (for he has but recently entered his fourteenth year), is reared under this excellent training, no one is better qualified to judge than yourself. He will shortly finish the Ethic, which will be followed by the Rhetoric of Aristotle, so that this labour that you have undertaken seems to offer you not merely a favourable, but even a providential opportunity: for I believe that it has not happened but by God's special providence that this highest exercise of your ability, judgment, and learning should be employed to polish so extraordinary a summit of royal majesty."

The following is an extract of a letter to Bullinger from Martin Micronius, one of the ministers of the German Church in London, dated 20th May, 1550 :—

"Our King is a youth of such godliness as to be a wonder to the whole world. He orders all things for the advancement of God's glory. He has, on every

Lord's day, a sermon such as he used to have during
Lent. I wish the bishops and nobility were inflamed
with the like zeal."[*]

Micronius, in a letter to Bullinger, of date 28th
August, 1550, explains a very important step in the
progress of the Reformation. The oath of supremacy
in the first Prayer Book of Edward VI., 1549, ended
with the words, 'So. help me God, all Saints, and the
Holy Evangelists.' In the second edition of 1552, the
words objected to were struck out, and the words retained were simply these—'So help me God, through
Jesus Christ.'

"The King, as you know, has nominated Hooper
to the bishopric of Gloucester, which, however, he
refused to accept unless he could be altogether re-
lieved from all appearance of popish superstition. Here
then a question immediately arises as to the form of
the oath which the bishops have ordered to be taken in
the name of God, the Saints, and the Gospels, which
impious oath Hooper positively refused to take. So,
when he appeared before the King in the presence of
the Council, Hooper convinced the King by many
arguments that the oath should be taken in the name of
God alone, who knoweth the heart. This took place on
the 20th July. It was so agreeable to the godly
King, that with his own pen he erased the clause of the
oath which sanctioned swearing by any creatures.
Nothing could be more godly than this act, or more
worthy of a Christian King."[†]

* Zurich Letters, Vol. III. p. 561, Parker Society.
† Zurich Letters, Vol. III. p. 566, Parker Society.

Rudolph Gualter, in a letter to Queen Elizabeth in 1559, wrote thus :—

"King Edward, your brother, of most pious memory, when scarcely out of his boyhood, was an object of admiration to all kingdoms by reason of his remarkable zeal for godliness and the restoration of religion, and bravely overthrew the tyranny of Antichrist throughout his realm. By which example God would shew that Antichrist has very little, or rather no strength to defend his kingdom, as soon as the light of the Divine Word has dispersed the darkness in which he is wont to hide himself. But because our ingratitude deserved it, a just God took to himself in peace our most godly King, as he did Josias of old, that he might not see the dreadful dispersion of religion, which would doubtless have appeared more painful to him than death itself."[*]

At the suggestion of Bishop Ridley, King Edward founded no less than sixteen grammar schools, and designed, if his life had been spared, to erect twelve colleges for the education of youth. Shortly before his death he sent for the bishop, and after thanking him for the sermon in which the bishop had strongly pressed the duty of providing for the relief of poverty and the ignorance of our fellow-men, added: "I took myself to be especially touched by your speech, as well in regard of the abilities God hath given me, as in regard of the example which from me He will require; for as in the kingdom I am next under God,

[*] Zurich Letters, Vol. III. p. 6, Ed. Parker Society.

so must I most nearly approach Him in goodness and mercy; for as our miseries stand most in need of aid from Him, so are we the greatest debtors—debtors to all that are miserable, and shall be the greatest accountants of our dispensation therein; and therefore, my lord, as you have given me, I thank you, this general exhortation, so direct me (I pray you), by what particular actions I may this way best discharge my duty."

Fuller, in his *Mixt Contemplations in Better Times*, relates that, "A covetous courtier complained to King Edward the Sixth, of Christ College in Cambridge, that it was a superstitious foundation, consisting of a master and twelve fellows, in imitation of Christ and his twelve apostles. He advised the King also to take away one or two fellowships, so to discompose that superstitious number. 'Oh no,' said the King, 'I have a better way than that to mar their conceit, I will add a thirteenth fellowship unto them;' which he did accordingly, and so it remaineth unto this day."

King Edward has noted in his journal that he fell sick of the measles and the small-pox on 2 April, 1552. His sickness must have been of a mild form, as it appears that he was restored to health before the end of the month of May.

A few months after his recovery, he again fell sick of a cough, and at the beginning of the February following, it had increased and had become very distressing. Neither regimen nor medicine could afford any relief. The cough continued to increase, accompanied with weakness and faintness. After a consultation of the physicians, they delivered their opinion, that the King was sick of consumption, and the disease was mortal. On the sixteenth of June the King's illness was of such a·character that there was no further hope of his recovery, and the physicians thought he could not survive the month of August.

At Greenwich, on the evening of the 6th day of July, 1553, in the seventeenth year of his age and in the seventh year of his reign, King Edward VI. died. At the time of his departure, there were present in his chamber, two gentlemen of the Privy Chamber, Sir Thomas Wrothe and Sir Henry Sidney, Doctor Owen and Doctor Wendy, also Christopher Salmón, his groom, who had been one of the King's personal attendants during the whole of his reign. Sir Henry Sidney has left on record the following account of the last service of duty and affection he performed during the last moments of his master.

"This young Prince, who died in my arms, had almost caused death to penetrate his dart even into my own soul; for to behold him, and how like a lamb he departed this life, and when his voice had left him, still he erected his eyes to heaven; it would have converted the fiercest of Papists if they had any grace in them of true faith in Christ. He would call upon none saving his Saviour. He prayed that God would be pleased to bestow the Gospel on his subjects for his glory and their salvation; he also in his sickness made a prayer to God to deliver this nation from that uncharitable religion of Popery, which was the chiefest cause for his election of the Lady Jane Grey to succeed before his sister Mary, though she was the heiress-apparent to his succession,—not out of spleen unto his sister for her religion, but out of pure love to his subjects, that he desired they might live, and die in the Lord as he did."

Foxe* has recorded—" As the time approached when it pleased Almighty God to call this young king from us, about three hours before his death, this godly child, his eyes being closed, speaking to himself, and thinking none to have heard him, made this prayer as followeth :—

" Lord God, deliver me out of this miserable and wretched life, and take me among thy chosen: how-beit, not my will, but thy will be done. Lord, I com-mit my spirit to Thee. O Lord, thou knowest how happy it would be for me to be with Thee; yet, for thy chosen's sake, send me life and health, that I may truly serve Thee. O my Lord God, bless thy people, and save thine inheritance. O Lord God, save thy chosen people of England. O my Lord God, defend this realm from papistry, and maintain thy true religion ; that I and my people may praise thy Holy Name, for thy Son, Jesus Christ's sake."

* Memorials, Vol. II., part I., pp. 35, 36.

EDWARD Sixiesme
de ce nom, par la grace
de dieu roy d'angleterre,
France et Irlande, Defen-
deur de la foy, et en
terre apres dieu chef de
l'église d'angleterre èt Irlande, A son trescher
et bien aymé Oncle
Edouard Duc de So-
merset Gouverneur de

sa personne, et Protecteur
de ses Royaumes, Pais
et subjectz.

Apres avoir considéré
(trescher et bien aymé oncle)
combien ceux desplaisent
a dieu qui despendent
tout leur temps en folies
et vanitéz de ce monde,
comme en passe temps
frivoles et jeux desquelz

2

ne vient prouffit et utili-
té, ny a soymesme, ny au
gendre humain, je me suis
amusé a faire quelque œu-
vre, lequel me sera (comme
j'espere) proufitable et a
vous aussy acceptable.   Puis,
donc, que voions beaucoup
de Papistes, non seulement
nous mauldire, mais ap-
peller et nommer héréti-
ques, pourtant qu' avons

3

delaissé leur Antichrist, avec
ses traditions, et ensuyvy
la lumiére qui nous est mon-
treé de dieu, nous sommes
esmeuz de faire quelque
œuvre pour nous defen-
dre de leurs contumelies,
et les mettre sur leur mesme dos.   Car ilz nous
appellent hérétiques, mais
euxmesmes le sont, puis
qu' ilz laissent la pure

4

voix de l'evangile, et suyvent
leur mesmes phantasies ;
comme il appert de ce que
Boniface troiesme de ce nom
(quand il estoit fuict évesque
universel) pensa en soymesme que ceste déféction la
de laquelle Paul parle en
la seconde épistre aux
Thessalon. deuxiesme chapitre,
fust avenue en soy.   Car S.
Paul dit Aussi mes freres

nous vous prions par l'ad-
venement de nostre seigneur
que ne soiez tost esmeuz
en vostre entendement, et que
ne soyez troublez, ny par esprit, ny parolle, ny epistre, comme si
la journée de Christ estoit
pres.   Que nul ne vous sé-
duise aucunement : car le jour
ne viendra point que pré-
miérement ne soit venu un
departement, et que l'homme

6

de peché ne soit revélé : le
filz de perdition, et l' ad-
versaire de dieu : et s'eslévera
sus tout jusques a estre assis
au temple de dieu, etc.
Toutesfois il suivit sa mesme phantasie, et ne se
detourna pas de son erreur,
lequel il scavoit estre bien
mauvais. Veu, donc, que
j' aperçoy par voz faictz
que vous avéz une grande

affection vers la parolle divine et syncere religion, je vous dedie cest œuvre present, vous priant de le prendre en gré. Dieu vous donne sa grace perpetuelle, et vous monstre sa bénignité pour tousjours. De mon palais de Ouestmester lez Londres, ce pénultime jour d'Aoust
1549.

PETIT TRAITÉ A
lencontre de la primauté
du pape.

NOUS pouvons tres bien voir et appercevoir par l'experience du monde,
que la nature humaine est prompte
a tous maux, et embrouillee de tous
vices : car quel pais y a il au monde
auquel n'y ait quelque vice et abus :
et principalement au temps present
veu que maintenant le grand empire

9

d'Antichrist est en vogue : lequel est la
source de tout mal : fontaine de tout a-
bomination, et vray filz du diable : pource-
que quand Dieu eut envoyé son filz
unique pour nostre infirmité, acellefin
de reconciler le monde a soy par la
mort d'iceluy, le diable changea deslors
les institutions de Christ en traditions
humaines, et pervertit les escritures a
son propos par le pape son ministre.
Et pourtant si les Astrologues (lesquelz
prouvent que toute chose retournera
a son element) disent la verité, le pape
descendra en enfer : car il ne pœut-

10

estre de Dieu pourtant que souz préten- 2 Corin. 11. A.
ce de religion et commandement de dieu
il a usurpé a soymesme l'authorité de
Christ : laquelle chose est veuë en tous
ses œuvres.   Parquoy il m'a semble le
mieux en ce livre de condamner premierement la papauté, et apres, la doctrine d'iceluy pape : Toutesfois c'est
une chose difficile, pourtant qu'il y a
beaucoup qui y contredisent : cenonobstant nous condamnerons la supéri-
orité du pape par les raisons ensui-
vantes.

11

La Premiere Partie.

Premierement la ou les papistes disent
que Romme est la mere de toutes eglises,
et pourtant que l'evesque de Romme
doit estre le supérieur ; Je respons qu'il
est impossible, entant que la premiere
promesse estoit faite au peuple Judai-
que : et aussy que Romme estoit infi-
dele, quand Jerusalem estoit fidele : car
Rom. 11. B. Paul, ecrivaut aux Rommains, dit,
Quand les Juifz tomboient, salut venoit entre les Gentilz.   Mais pourtant que les papistes ne pevent

12

prouver que Romme est la mere de toutes autres églises, ilz disent que l'evesque de Romme a reçeu son povoir de
Pierre, auquel estoit donnée la mesme
authorité de Christ, laquelle ledit evesque a maintenant, et taschent de le
prouver par ces textes ensuivans, Tu   Math. 16. C.
es Pierre, et dessus ceste pierre j'edifieray mon eglise, dit Christ à Pierre :   Et
un peu apres, je te donray les clefz
du ciel; et aussy ilz alleguent ce lieu
ou Pierre dit à Christ je t'ayme Sei-   Jan. 21. E.
gneur : car ilz disent que celuy qui
ayme Christ est le principal, et que

13

Pierre aymoit Christ le mieux de tous, et pourtant qu'il est le principal. D'avantage ilz afferment qu'il estoit commandé a luy seul de paistre les brebis, et d'estre les pescheur des hommes ; et qu'il parloit le premier, et respondoit à Jesus, Voicy deux glaives ; lequel lieu les papistes interpretent que Pierre avoit une

Luc. 22. E. espée temporelle, et l'autre spirituelle. Ilz alleguent aussy aucunes raissons humaines, que comme les mouches à miel ont un roy, ainsi tous les Chrestiens doivent avoir un pape : et que comme au temps passé il y avoit un évesque principal entre

14

les Juifz (comme Moses et Aaron)
aussy que maintenant un evesque des
evesques est necessaire.   Il y a deux
grandes menteries en peu de parolles :
l'une est, que l'authorité de la supre-
mité de l'eglise estoit donnée à Pierre,
l'autre que Pierre estoit a Romme.
Pour le premier, ou ilz disent que ceste
authorité luy estoit donné par ces
motz, Tu ca pierre et sur ceste, etc.
Je respons que, si vous regardéz la chose precedente, et ensuivante, vous voir-
réz que Christ ne parloit pas de pierre
entant qu'il estoit nomme, mais entant

Exod. 4. D.

Math. 16. C.

15

qu'il estoit fidele : car le précedent est que
Pierre disoit, Tu es le filz de Dieu ; par
quoy il est évident que Christ ne disoit
pas que Pierre estoit le fondement de
l'eglise, mais qu'il parloit de la foy de
Pierre. L'ensuivant est que Dieu ap-
pelloit Pierre, Satan : mais l'eglise de
Christ n'est pas fondée dessus Satan,
et pourtant elle n'est pas fondée dessus
Pierre : Car si l'eglise estoit fondée dessus
Pierre, elle auroit un feible fondement :

Math. 7. D. et tout ainsi qu'une maison laquelle a
un fondement débile ne pœut demeu-
rer long temps mais tombe, ainsy

:.   16

l'eglise ayant si pauvre fondacion que
Pierre est, et si debile, ne pourroit de-
meurer, mais tomberoit tout inconti-
nent. Par lesquelles choses on pœut
voir que ce texte, Tu es Pierre, et dessus
ceste pierre j'edifieray mon eglise, doit
estre entendu, que sur la foy de Pierre,
nompas dessus lui est l'eglise fondée :
pource qu'il estoit un vaisseau fragile
et fort debile : car il renioit Christ par
trois fois. Le second texte est que les   Math. 16. G.
clefz du ciel estoient données a Pierre.   Marc. 8. C.
Je respons que les clefz estoient don-
nées, non seulement a Pierre, mais

17

aussy aux autres apostres : et par cest
argument je respons qu'il n'estoit pas
le principal : car les autres recevoient
la mesme authorité de clefz, laquelle
lui est commise : Pour laquelle chose
Galat. 2. B. Paul appelle Pierre la Coulomne, nompas le fondement, d'eglise, et son com-
pagnon, nompas son governeur : car
quelles sont les clefz du ciel ? l'authorité de pardonner les peches ? non :
mais le preschement de l'évangile de
Dieu le pere ; ouy, bien de Dieu, nompas
du pape ou diable. Et tout ainsi que
quand l'huys est ouvert quiconque

veult pœut entrer, ainsy quand Dieu
envoyoit son sincere commandement et
son évangile ilz ouvroient la vérité la   2 Coria. 2. D.
quelle est la porte du ciel, et donnoient
aux hommes a entendre l'ecriture la
quelle s'ilz suivent, ils seront sauvéz.
Parquoy on pœut entendre que l'evangile
et la vérité de l'écriture sont les seules
portes qui conduisent l'homme au royaume de Dieu. Pour laquelle chose saint
Paul dit, Quiconque invoquera le nom   Rom. 10. C.
de Dieu sera sauvé. Comment invo-
queront ilz celuy auquel ilz ne croient
pas ? Comment croiront ilz en celuy

duquel ilz n'ont pas ouy parler ? Comment orront ilz sans avoir vu un prescheur ?
Rom. 4. A. Et un peu apres il dit. Foy vient par ouïr,
et ouyr de la parolle de Dieu. Au quatriesme chapitre aux Rommains aussi
il dit. A celuy qui n'œuvre pas, mais
croit en celuy qui justifie les meschans,
sa foy luy est imputée a justice.
Maintenant nous prouverons que le
preschement de l'évangile est la clef
du ciel. Au huitiesme chapitre aux
Rommains (comme j'ay dessus dit)
Paul affirme que quiconque invoque le
nom du Seigneur est sauvé, et que le pres-

20

chement de l'évangile est l'entrée en l'invocation de Dieu : adonc il s'ensuit que le preschement de l'evangile est l'entrée du salut. D'avantage Paul affirme que foy justifie, et que le preschement de l'evangile fait la foi (laquelle chose j'ay demonstrée icy devant) pourtant il s'ensuit que le vray preschement est l'entrée en justification ; car tout ainsy qu'une terre sémée poeut produire fruit pourveu que la semence ne soit semée en terre pleine de chardons, brieres ou pierres : et encor s'elle est sémée en telle terre elle fera la terre un peu meilleu-

Math. 14. A.

Marc. 4. A.

Luc. 8. B.

21

BIBLIOTECA NAZIONALE
ROMA

re, ainsy si le commandement de Dieu
est semé a cueur d'honnestes gens, ou de
ceux que ont un bon zele a la vérité,
il les confermera en toute bonté : mais
si ancuns sont obstinez et opiniatres,
ilz ne pevent imputer la faute a l'ecriture, veu qu'elle est en euxmesmes.
Pourtant nous nous devons efforcer que

Math. 28. E. l'evangile soit preschée par tout le monde,
Marc. 16. D. comme il est écrit.   Tout povoir m'est
donné en la terre at au ciel, pourtant

Luc. 14. G. allez et preschez a toutes creatures,
les baptisans en mon nom.
Puis donc qu'il est prouvé que les clefz

du ciel sont l'authorité de prescher : et
que l'authorité de prescher estoit donnée   Math. 16. C.
a chacun apostre, je ne puis voir comme
par ce texte, l'authorité estoit donnée a
Pierre plus qu'aux autres : car Paul dit
qu'il est aussey bon que quelqu'un des
autres apostres ; laquelle chose, s'elle est
vraye, Pierre n'estoit pas meilleur que
luy : et s'on me demandoit lequel des
deux est le meilleur, je dirois que Paul
est le meilleur, pourtant qu'il preschoit
le plus de tous.   Mais nous devons te-
nir pour certain que l'esprit de Dieu   Galat. 2. A.
tomboit entre tous, et que le mesme   Actes 2. A.

esprit de Dieu qui estoit en Pierre estoit
aussi en Paul : par laquelle chose on
pœut prouver que nul d'eux fust supérieur de l'autre.   Puis les papistes
Jan. 21. H. disent que quand Christ estoit resus-
cité de mort a vie, il demanda qui l'aymoit, et que Pierre respondoit qu'il
l'aymoit : et pourtant (comme ilz disent)
qu'il est le principal.   Mais s'ainsy est,
adonc chacun honneste homme doit
avoir la suprémité dessus tous autres : pourtant que chacun qui est bon
et honneste ayme Dieu : car cela est le
point et office de chacun vray Chrestien.

24

Or la question n'est pas, si Pierre estoit
fidele, honneste, bon, saint ou vray
Chrestien ; mais s'il estoit le principal
chef, gouverneur, et roy par dessus
tous autres : ou s'il estoit meilleur que
les autres apostres et ministres de
Jesus Christ : car si le pape vouloit a-
voir l'authorité de Pierre, laquelle est
de prescher, je serois content : mais il
ne fait rien moins que le commandement de Dieu : car Jesus s'enfuioit
quand les Juifs taschoient a le faire   Jan. 6. D.
roy, et empereur : mais le pape par
violence ou a tort ou a travers assub-

jétit a soy toutes nations. Jesus avoit
une coronne d'espines, et une robe de

Math. 27. C. pourpre, et estoit moqué de tout chacun : mais le pape a trois couronnes
et est honoré des rois, des princes, des
empereurs, et de tous estatz. Jesus

Jan. 14. A. lave les piedz des ses apostres : mais les
rois baisent les piedz du pape. Jesus

Math. 17. D. paië tribut : mais le pape reçoit et ne

Math. 8. A. paie nul tribut. Jesus presche et le
pape se repose en son chasteau de Saint

Luc. 6. B. Ange. Jesus remedie aux maladies :
mais le pape se resjouit du sang respan-

Jan. 19. C. du. Christ porte sa croix : mais le

26

pape est porté. Christ venoit en paix   Luc. 2. A.
comme un pauvre homme au monde :
mais le pape prend grand plaisir a
mettre guerre entre les rois et princes de la terre. Christ vient dessus
un pauvre asne humblement, et plein   Math. 21. B.
de pitie : mais le pape vient en toute
pompe (combien qu'apres le beau temps
vient la pluië). Christ est un agneau :   Jan. 1. C.
mais le pape est un loup. Christ estoit
pauvre : et le pape veult avoir souz son   Luc. 9. A.
povoir tous les royaumes de Chresti-
enté. Christ jetta hors du temple les   Jau. 2. B.
changeurs, et ceux qui vendoient : lesquelz

· 27

Math. 21. B. le pape reçoit. Jesus ordonne la cene

Marc. 11. C. en memoire de soy : et le pape inventoit

Luc. 22. B. la messe maitresse de toute abusion.

Marc. 16. D. Jesus monte au ciel, et le pape tombe en enfer. Dieu commande que nous

Deut. 6. A. n'ayons quelque autre Dieu que luy :

Exod. 20. A. mais le pape veult estre honoré comme

Math. 4. B. un grand Dieu. Dieu nous a deffen-

Baruc. 6. A. du de commettre idolatrie : mais le pape est l'autheur de tous ymages. Dieu

Exod. 20. A. nous a defendu de jurer en vain : mais le pape a donné congé a tous ceux qui sont ses amis de se perjurer. Dieu

Math. 12. B. nous a commandé d'observer les jours

28

de festes, en priant, lisant, ou estudiant :
et le pape passe ce jour la en pompe,
et jouant, en oysiveté, et en hurlant ou
abayant en l'eglise.   Dieu a deffendu de tuer quelqu'un : et c'est grand pitie de voir comme le pape persécute les
Chrestiens : mais Dieu nous a predit
de ceste persécution au vingt et quatriesme chapitre de Mathieu, Beaucoup
de faux prophetes (dit Christ) seront en
ce temps la : Iniquité sera grande, et   Math. 24. A.
charité s'en ira : mais l'evangile sera
presché a toute creature ; pourtant
quand vous verrez l'abomination

au saint lieu predit de Daniel le prophete, adonc ceux que sont en Jerusalem s'enfuiront aux montaignes.

N'est ce pas ainsi maintenant ? ouy : car il y a beaucoup de loups vestus de peaux de brebis : lesquels souz pretence de religion obscurissent la vraie doctrine de Christ : et toute l'abomination estoit quasi au lieu saint, c'est a dire au temple de Dieu.

Or pour retourner au propos, Dieu a deffendu adultere : mais pourtant que le pape veult estre obeisant a son pere Satan, il commande que les pre-

1 Corin. 5. A.

stres entretiennment beaucoup de conçu-
bines et putains, et que jamais ne se
joignent a quelqu'une en mariage.
Dieu a deffendu de dérober quelque
homme, femme ou enfant : mais le pape
a esté si vieux larron que maintenant
il derobe l'honneur deu a Dieu, et le
transfere a soymesme. Dieu a deffendu de tesmoigner faussement alencontre
de quelqu'un : mais le pape dit, Tout
flaire bon, mais qu'argent vienne.
Dieu a commandé que nous fussions
contens de cela qui est nostre : mais le
pape veult que chacune maison luy

paie tribut : et pour concluire, il est en
toutes choses contraire a Dieu. Mais
je ne le puis blamer : car il fait la com-

Ephes. 6. D. mandement de Paul, qui dit, Filz soyez
obeissans à voz parens, et ainsi fait il :
car le diable nommé ypocrisie est son
pere, auquel il se monstre obeissant : et

1 Pier. 5. C. le diable va comme un lyon rugissant
pour decevoir le monde (comme saint
Pierre dit) et le pape ne fait il pas
ainsy ? ouy : car le pape ordonne
non seulement injustes et
mauvaises loix : mais aussy cherche
la mort d'un chacun qui a un bon

zele ou amour envers Dieu.   Or pour
venir à la primauté de Pierre je voudroie
bien congnoistre combien de royaumes
saint Pierre avait souz son empire : car
il estoit impossible qu'il eust tout souz
soy, veu que saint Jaques estoit evesque
de Jerusalem, laquelle cité estoit alors
Chrestienne.   Aussy je ne puis voir
comme Pierre seroit le principal : car
Paul dit que les apostres sont tretous   1 Corin. 4. D.
nostres : et que nous ne sommes a nul
sinon a Christ, et que Christ est a Dieu.
Semblablement Pierre ne s'appelle pas
par autre nom que l'apostre de Christ.   1 Pierre 1. A.

Par laquelle chose il est manifeste que nous ne sommes pas à Pierre, mais que Pierre est a nous. Davantage, quand

Gal. 2. B. Paul venoit en Antioche il resistoit a Pierre, laquelle chose il n'eust pas fait si Pierre eust esté en telle authorité qu'il ne povoit mentir (comme ils disent). Mais (comme j'ay dessus dit) Paul, voyant la dissimulation de Pierre, luy dit. Si tu estant Juif fais comme un Gentil, et nompas comme un Juif : pourquoy fais tu observer la maniere

Gal. 2. C. des Juifz aux Gentilz : nous que sommes par nature Juifz et nompas pe-

cheures des Gentilz : pourtant que nous
sçavons que nulle chair sera justifiée
par les œuvres de la loy : mais que
nous sommes justifiez par la foy en
Jesus christ, auquel nous avons mis
tout nostre espoir, acellefin d'estre justifiez par la foy, et nompas par la
loy, etc. Voions donc comme il
pœut estre que Pierre soit le principal :
car si celuy estoit le principal qui aime
mieux Christ, il appert que Jan seroit
le chef des autres : car Christ luy   Jan. 19. C.
bailla sa mere en garde : et aussi Jan
se couchoit entre les bras de Christ   Jan. 14. D.

quand il estoit a souper. Mais à
propos je demande s'il a quelque concile légitime sans que le pape le con-
voque ? Je sçay bien que les papistes
diront qu'il n'y en a nul. Adonc je
demande si le pape devant qu'il soit
eleu pœut convoquer un concile ? je
sçay bien qu'ilz diront qu'il ne pœut.
Si donc nul concile n'est legitime
sans le pape : et nul qui brigue pour
estre pape ne pœut convoquer un
concile, adonc le concile qui confer-
moit le pape d'estre superieur de l'egli- .
se n'est pas legitime ; pourtant qu'il

n'estoit pas convoqué du pape : pource
qu'alors il n'y en avoit point.
Maintenant qu'ilz ont esté repousez
de ceste raison, ils fuyent a un autre,
disans que Christ commandoit a Pierre
de paistre ses brebis : mais il comman- Jan. 21. E.
doit ainsy a tous les autres, disant,
Allez et preschéz a toutes nations, les Math. 28. C.
baptisans en mon nom : mais le pa-
pe ne fait pas le commandement de
Christ: car il ne paist pas les brebis,
mais les devore, et mange comme
un lyon rugissant qui cherche sa 1 Pier. 5. C.
proye pour devorer les petis.   Or je

37

voudrois que le pape fist le commandement que Dieu donna à Pierre : car
je ne suis pas marry pourtant qu'il
a ceste authorité de prescher Christ a
tout le monde : mais pourtant qu'il
laisse la prédication de l'évangile et
usurpe a soymesme l'authorité
laquelle de droit appartient a Christ,
c'est d' estre le primat de l'église.
Il est vray que le pape est primat de
l'eglise, nompas divine ou catholique,
mais diabolique : car il transgresse le
commandement donné a Pierre et aux
autres apostres en general : pourtant

que quand Christ envoyoit ses douze Math. 10. A.
apostres pour prescher l'evangile de pe-
nitence et le royaume de Dieu, il leur
disoit. Alléz vous en, et soyéz comme
brebis entre les loups : mais l'évesque
de Romme est comme un loup entre
les brebis : car il devore et mange toutes les pauvres brebis de Christ : et quand
elles se sont cachées de paour quelles
ont, adonc il feint la voix d'une brebis acellefin de les manger. Il se pœut
excuser disant que prescher est trop
vile office pour luy, et qu'il a des offi-
ciers, et ministres : mais qu'il doit ouir

chanter les messes.   Je respons pour
la premiere partie, veu que l'office de prescher
n'estoit pas trop vile pour pierre, le
quel avoit receu son povoir et
authorité de Christ, il me semble que
ceux la qui se disent les successeurs
de pierre, ne doivent penser que ceste
office est trop vile pour eux.

1 Tim. 7. A. Saint Paul dit a Timothée quel chacun evesque doit estre.   Un evesque
(dit Paul) doit estre irrépréhensible
le mary d'une seule femme, sobre,
sage, biengarny de vertu, chaste, lo-
geant les pauvres, apte a enseigner,

nompas yvrongne, malfaiteur, noisif
ny desireux des biens d'autruy : mais
il doit estre bon governeur de sa fa-
mille, ayant ses filz souz soy en chasteté. Maintenant nous ajournerons
le pape devant Saint Paul, et verrons
s'il est coupable au non, selon la reigle
de Saint Paul. Le premier commandement lequel un evesque doit observer
est d'estre irrépréhensible : mais nous
avons prouvé que l'evesque de Romme
transgresse tous les commandemens de
Dieu, pour laquelle chose il est coupable. Le second est qu'il soit le mary

41

d'une femme, en laquelle chose l'evesque
de Romme fault beaucoup : car il entre-
tient des putains, et pense que mechante fornication est meilleure que bon et honneste mariage. Le troisiesme est qu'il
soit sobre, sage, biengarny de vertus,
et chaste ; desquelles choses l'evesque de
Romme n'observe nulles. Le quatriesme est qu'il soit liberal, et loge les pauvres : mais l'evesque de Romme est plein
de toute avarice. Le cinquiesme est qu'il
soit apte a enseigner : mais nostre diable, ou pere diabolique pense que de
maintenir la gloire de Dieu, et pres-

cher, est trop vile office pour luy ; toutesfois son prédécesseur Pierre preschoit
l'evangile, ou autrement il pechoit a.
lencontre de Dieu, en ce qu'il n'obser-
voit pas ce commandement, Allez et   Math. 28. C.
preschez l'evangile a tout le monde ;   Jan. 21. E.
cenonobstant pour sa mesme commo-
dité il veult emprisonner, tuer, bruler,
celuy qui presche la parolle, et veult
luymesme estre.le bourreau, s'il n'en
povoit trouver quelque autre : parquoy
nous voyous qu'il s'ayme mieux qu'il
ne fait Dieu.   Que diray plus ?   Il
transgresse tout l'ordre de saint Paul.

43

Dites maintenant s'il est coupable ou,
ou non. Or nous respondrons a
leur argumens, Que Pierre est le Principal : Ilz disent que Pierre estoit commandé de paistre les brebis : je respons qu' a tous les apostres leur estoit
aussy commandé de paistre les brebis
en cecy, Allez preschans, etc. Mais ce n'est
rien autre chose de paistre les brebis,
sinon de prescher l'evangile. Aussy
leur autre argument est de la mesme
substance, quand ilz disent que Pierre
estoit le pescheur des hommes :
car Andry et Jan estoient aussy pes-

44

cheurs des hommes : et ce n'est rien
autre chose d'estre pescheur des hommes, qu' estre prescheur de Christ.
Or si la prédication de nul
n'est légitime sans l'authorité
de Pierre ou de pape, adonc la prédication de saint Paul n'estoit pas légitime, laquelle il n'a pas receu de Pierre.   Cenonobstant le pape pense
estre un Dieu, disant, Je ne puis mentir : pourtant ce que j'ay dit est vray.
Mais acela je respons que s'il n'est
meilleur que Pierre il pœut mentir :
car Pierre renioit Christ par troys   Math. 26. G.

fois : adonc Pierre mentoit trois fois.
Aussy Paul le reprouvoit pour sa

Gal. 2. C. dissimulation. Mais l'evesque de
Romme ment grandement, quand
ce ne seroit en autre chose sinon qu'il
se dit chef de l'eglise Chrestienne, et
avoir les clefz du ciel : car si le pape
avoit les clefz du ciel, je demande
ceste question. Quand le pape est
mort, et nul autre a les clefz, comment en-
treront les ames au ciel ? car personne n'a les clefz s'il n'est pape :
Adonc il avient que quand le pape

46

est mort, les huis du ciel sont fermez ;
Mais c'est une folle chose de dire que
le pape a les clefz du ciel, et d'enfer :
car Christ est nostre seul médiateur,   1 Timo. 2. A.
nostre porte, nostre chef,
nostre pasteur, nostre redempteur, et
souverain maistre : lequel (après qu'il
eut enseigné, fait des miraclés, souffert   Math. 27. A.
mort et passion pour tous fideles, donné   Marc. 16. B.
salut a tout chacun qui croit en luy, et   Luc. 24. B.
par sa mort pense fidelement estre sauvé,)   Jan. 19. C.
monta au ciel en toute gloire et honneur,   Math. 28. D.
et se sied a la dextre de son pere, pri-   Marc. 16. D.
ant pour nous : lequel aussi demourra   Luc. 24. E.

47

Jan. 21. C. la avec son pere et le saint esprit, un en
Math. 26. A. deité, trois en personnes: plein de toute
vertu, et exempt de tout vice, estant a-
Eph. 1. C. vec nous en esprit et par tout comme son
Ebre. 4. A. pere, jusques au temps qu'il viendra ju-
Math. 25. B. ger le monde au jour de jugement : la bonté
duquel est invisible : la misericorde du-
quel est inénarrable : la gloire duquel est
inéstimable. Iceluy est nostre gouverneur
Paul. 24. A. et maistre : iceluy est nostre berger : iceluy
Jan. 10. A. est nostre redempteur : nous sommes ses
subjetz et brebis : nous sommes rache-
téz par luy, et lavéz de l'eau de baptesme, pour signification que nous sommes

48

ses brebis.   Nul autre n'est nostre pasteur,
gouverneur, ny pope : car si quelqu'autre
estoit nostre chef, nous serions un monstre
ayant deux testes.   Paul écrivant aux
Corinthiens dit que tout est nostre : et que
Pierre, Apollo, et tout les autres apostres   1 Corin. 4. D.
sont nostres, et nous a Christ, et Christ a
Dieu.   Parquoy il appert que Pierre n'est
pas nostre chef, mais nostre ministre.
Pourtant nous devons penser que Dieu est
nostre pere spirituel, qui oste pas sa passion
toutes les peines de mort et d'enfer a tous
ceux qui se fient eu luy : car a luy nous
crions, Abba pere : Donc si le pape veult   Rom. 8. C.

estre appelle pere spirituel, nous avons trois
peres en tout : desquelz l'un est charnel, et
deux spirituelz. Mais j'ause dire que si le
diable n'est nostre pere spirituel, le pape
aussi ne l'est pas : car comme Christ est
l'Agneau immaculé, et l'unique filz de dieu
plein de toute vertu, ainsi au contraire, le
pape est un ord villain loup, et l'unique
filz du diable son pere : duquel il a receu
toute son authorité et office. Mais je voudrois bien sçavoir si le pape est nostre pere
spirituel, charnel, ou diabolique. Premiére-
ment, charnel, il ne le pœut estre : pourtant
qu'il professe chasteté, et n'est point marié.

Aussy il ne pœut pas estre spirituel, pourtant qu'il est adonné au monde : adonc
il s'eusuit qu'il est le pere diabolique.
Or concluons que comme il estoit dit de
Christ, Tu es mon filz, je t'ay engendré   Pſal. 2. D.
aujourd'huy, Dieu dira ainsy du pape,
Tu es mon ennemy, je t'ay destruit aujourd'huy : et que comme Christ estoit de .
l'ordre de Melchisedech, ainsi le pape est   Pſal. 110. A.
de l'ordre diabolique. Mais comme Chre-
stienté est spirituellement tresbonne, et est
bien formée en esprit, ainsi s'il n'y a bon ordre pour la conserver, elle est destruite :
car tout ainsi que le corps d'un homme ne

pœut estre sain, s'il a deux testes, ou quatre
bras, ou quatre piedz, ainsy ces pais de
Chrestienté ne pevent estre bien en ordre
s'ilz ont deux qui dominent, et ayent l'empire de tout le monde.   Maintenant on mè
diroit, donc vous ne vouléz pas qu'il y ait
des rois, et empereurs : je respons que Dieu
Math. 1. B.   qui a envoyé son filz unique en terre icy
Psal. 110. A.   bas, l'a fait roy de la terre, en spirituelle
et temporelle authorité.   Celuy en son em-
pire a mis des rois, lesquelz sont ses lieutenans : mais il n'en a ordonné nul pour son
grand evesque : car il n'est pas ainsi ordonné
en la Sainte écriture. Or, si les papistes disent

52

que le pape est son héritier, je voudroye
qu'il attendist jusques a ce que Christ mou-
rust, affin d'avoir son royaume : pourtant
que les héritiers ont l'heritage apres
la mort de leur prédecesseurs.
Maintenant les papistes disent que comme
en la vieille loy il y avoit un arcevesque   Exod 4. C.
du peuple Israelite ainsy maintenant il y
doit avoir un chef principal en la Chrestienté.   Je respons que la prestrice d'Aaron
et Moses representoit la primauté nompas du pape, mais de Christ ; lequel vint
en terre et souffrit mort pour nous autres :   Math. 1. C.
car Christ dit de soymesme qu'il est

Jan. 4. D. nostre Messias ; et aussi qu'il est le vray
Jan. 6. D. pain descendant du ciel : et qu'il est nostre
seul berger : car comme Jan testifie, il disoit,
Jan. 10. A. certes je vous dy que celui qui n'entre
par moi en l'estable des brebis, mais vi-
Prover. 11. D. ent par ailleurs, il est larron : car celuy
que entre par l'huis est le berger : celuy qui
garde l'huis luy ouvre, et les brebis ont
ouy sa voix et il appelle ses brebis, et s'en
va devant elles, et les brebis le suivent
pourtant qu'elles congnoissent sa voix, et
autre elles ne suivront. Donc le pape,
qui ne vient pas de par Christ, est un a-
bominable larron : pour laquelle chose

54

toutes vrayes et honnestes brebis doivent
s'en partir de luy : car il vient pour les
devorer, et nompas pour les paistre ;
pour les engloutir, et nompas pour les
enseigner. Maintenant, puis-
que les papistes sont batus de leur mesme baston (cela est de leur mesme argument) ilz disent qu'apres que les disciples de Christ avoient presché long
temps ilz retournoient a Jesus, lequel
leur demanda s'ilz avoient eu quelque
glaive tout ce temps la, et qu'ilz disoient,
voicy deux glaives. Or ilz disent
que l'un signifie le povoir temporel, et

l'autre le spirituel : laquelle raison (comme il sera demonstré icy apres) est sotte et vaine. Car premierement nous devons considerer de quel lieu les apostres venoient : car ilz avoient esté envoyés pour prescher Christ a toutes nations, et demonstrer la lumiere a ceux qui estoient en tenebres. Secondement nous devons considerer quel povoir Christ avoit en la terre. Il dit que son royaume n'est pas de ce monde : car il y a deux manieres d'authorité, l'une spirituelle et l'autre temporelle. Pour laquelle chose Saint Paul en sa pre-

Marc. 6. A.

Luc. 9. A.

56

miére epistre aux Corinthiens dit que 1 Corin. 12. B.
comme il y a au corps divers membres
pour diverses causes, ainsy il y a en l'egliso
de Christ aucuns ministres spirituelz, comme apostres, prophetes, et docteurs : et
aucuns temporelz, comme rois, empereurs,
gouverneurs, et lieutenans. Or Christ
estoit ministre spirituel, comme il dit soy
mesme, disant, Mon royaume n'est pas de
ce monde. Et aussi quand deux freres
venoient a luy le requerant de diviser Luc. 12. B.
leur héritage, il respondoit, Qui m'a
fait juge entre vous ? La troisiesme
chose laquelle doit estre consideree, est

57

que Christ parloit en moquerie.   La
quatriesme, que tous les apostres disoient ensemble, voicy deux glaives.
La cinquiesme chose est que les apostres
n'entendoient pas ce que Christ disoit.
Par toutes ces choses cy nous povons
facilement entendre ce texte : car apres
que les disciples estoient envoyéz pour
prescher l'evangile de vérité, ilz retournoient a Jesus, lequel leur disoit, Aviez
vous quelque espée tout ce temps ? comme
en voulant dire, Quand je vous envoi-
ois vous vouliez avoir des bastons avec
vous : maintenant que pensez vous, ma

grace ne vous a elle pas gardée de tout
mal? ou autrement, Aviez vous quelque
besoing d'avoir espée? Adonc les disciples
(et nompas Pierre seul) lesquelz n'entendoient pas ce que Christ disoit, respondoient qu'ils avoient deux glaives.
Parquoy nous voyons que Christ parloit en moquerie, et que tous les disciples
respondoient, et nompas Pierre seul, comme en disant, J'ay deux espées, l'une qui
signifie ma temporelle authorité: et l'autre qui
signifie la spirituelle jurisdicti-
on. Aussy Christ ne povoit et
ne vouloit pas donner la temporelle au-

thorité, pourtant qu'il estoit ministre spirituel.   Mais les papistes faillent beaucoup en un argument : car ilz disent
que Cephas est un chef, ou en vérité
Cephas est une pierre.   Maintenant
(quand ceux cy leurs argumens sont affoi-
bliz) ilz disent qu'il est vray semblable
que Pierre estoit le chef, pourtant
qu'il parloit le premier : et au temps
dessus dit il respondoit pour tous :
Mais il est plus vray semblable qu'il
n'estoit pas le chef des autres, pourtant
2 Cor. 11. F. que Paul se dit n'estre inférieur a nul
12. D. des apostres : du nombre desquelz estoit

Pierre. Or nous ne devons dis-
puter maintenant quelle chose semble   ·
estre vraye, mais quelle chose est vraie
sans faute.   Toutesfois nous verrons s'il
est vray semblable ou non : car Andry
parloit aucunefois le premier : et ne doit
on douter que chacun d'eux ne parlast
aucunesfois le premier : mais il ne s'ensuit pas pourtant que qui parle le premier aucunesfois soit evesque des evesques : car entant qu' il parloit le premier cela signifie qu' il estoit d'une nature
pleine de courage ; on autrement qu'il
desiroit estre le plus grand : mais Christ

Math. 18. A.	dit, celuy que veult estre le plus grand
Luc. 1. E.	sera le plus petit entre vous. Ainsy il
8. C.	n'y a point d'orgueilleux tiltre en l'eglise
Rom. 12. C.	de Christ : car Dieu ayme humilité, et
Philip. 2. B.	dit que celuy qui reçoit un petit enfant
Jaques 4. B.	en son nom, le reçoit : et aussy que celuy
1 Pier. 5. B.	que n'est pas semblable a un enfant, ne
Marc. 9. B.	sera pas apte pour le royaume de Di-
	eu. Mais Pierre soymesme ne s'attri-
	bue pas si hault tiltre, que le pape attri-
1 Pier. 1. A.	bue a soymesme : car il dit, Pierre le apo-
	stre et serviteur de Jesus christ, et non
2 Pier. 1. A.	plus : mais le pape, que dit il ? " Paul ti-
	ers de ce nom, par la grace de Dieu

tressaint pere et pape, vicaire de Christ,
lieutenant de Pierre, Dieu en terre, evesque des evesques, prince de princes, et
roi des rois." Voyez icy comme il se
dit Dieu, et blaspheme Christ. Voyez
comme il est plein de toute magnificen-
ce et orgueil. Voyez comme il a un beau
tiltre et nom, combien qu'il soit un serpent
venimeux : car il se dit tressaint pere, la
ou il est un abominable larron, et conta-
miné de tout immundiceté. Il se dit pape, le quel mot signifie pere de toutes nations, la ou il les déstruit. Il se dit
vicaire de Christ, et lieutenant de saint

63

Pierre, et Dieu en terre, ou il est vicaire de Belzebub, lieutenant de Lucifer, et le diable terreste : car il semble estre bon, mais il est mauvais. Et comme saint Corin.11.D. Paul dit aux Corinthiens ; ce n'est pas merveille si les ministres du diable sont plaisans et triumphans à l'œil, veu que le diable soymesme se transforme en un ange de lumiére. pourtant vous pov-ez bien appercevoir les vrais ministres de la parolle, d'entre les faulx Antichrists pource que les vrais apostres cheminent selon l'esprit de Dieu : mais les faulx apostres cheminent selon la chair.

nous verrons donc si le pape est ministre
de Dieu ou du diable. Certainement il
est du diable, ce ay je grand paour : car il
se dit honneste homme, tressaint evesque,
roy des roys : la ou il' est tiran de tirans ;
car tous les autres tirans exerçoient leur
tirannie dessus les corps des gens, mais ce
diable, ce loup, ce tiran, exerce sa tirannie
dessus les ames, contreignant les pauvres
and simples agneaux de Dieu delaisser
leur foy, par laquelle ilz sont sauvéz, et   Gal. 2. C.
suivre ses abominables tradicions, et pre-   3. A.
ceptes diaboliques. Aussy s'ilz ne font
ses preceptes, c'est adire adorer des yma-

ges, offrir aux ydoles et diables, il les
brule ou leur fait faire amende honorable ou les gehenne et tourmente.

Du temps du feu roy mon pere quand
son nom fut effacé de livres, il estoup-
pa les bouches des Chrestiens avec ses
six articles, comme avec six poins.
Aussy maintenant en france devant
qu' on brule quelqu'un, on luy couppe
la langue un peu auparavant, a celle-
fin qu'il ne parle. Veu donc que le
pape est le ministre de Lucifer, j'ny bon
espoir que comme Lucifer tomboit
hors du ciel en enfer, ainsy que le pape

son vicaire tombera hors de ceste gloire de la papauté en grand dérision. Car David dit au pseaumes, que Dieu veult estre Psal. 18. C. pervers avec les pervers : et saint avec les saints. Or le pape a osté l'honneur a Dieu : pourtant j'ay bon espoir que Dieu luy ostera ses honneurs et sa gloire. Aussy marie mere de Christ a dit Luc. 1. K. que Dieu a osté la gloire des riches, et l'a donnée aux humbles. Pourtant (o pape) garde toy bien ; car si tu tombes tu auras une grand cheute. Et tout ainsi qu'un homme que est monté en une tour, s'il tombe il prendra un grand

sault, ainsi vous qui avéz monté jusque
aux cieux tomberéz jusque en enfer,

Math. 11. D. ainsy que Christ a prédit de Tyr et Sidon.
Mais pour venir à la primanté
du pape, je sçay bien que l'ecriture par-

Eph. 4. A. le d'un Dieu, d'une foy, d'un baptesme;

1 Corin. 8. A. mais nompas d'un pape.   Or si Pierre

1 Timot. 2 B. estoit Dieu en terre et vicaire de Christ

Math. 19. C. nous eussions esté baptiséz en sou nom :

Eph. 3. A. mais Paul (lequel dit qu'il n'est inféri-

2 Cor. 11. E. eur à nul des autres apostres) ne veult

12. D. pas que nous soyons baptiséz en son
nom : Et tant seulement ne veult il que

1 Corin. 1. B. nous soyons baptiséz au nom de Pierre,

68

mais aussy ne veult pas qu'on disse, Je
suis à Pierre je suis à Paul, je suis a Apollo.
Maintenant que les papistes ne
pevent prouver par l'ecriture que nous
devons avoir un pape, ilz ont recours
aux similitudes, disans. Tout ainsy que
les bestes de la terre (comme les mouches
à miel) ont un roy qui domine sur elles,
ainsy tous Chretiens doivent avoir
un roy et pape : alaquelle raison je res-
pondray en trois manieres. Prémiere-
ment leur raison n'est pas extraite de la
sancte escriture, mais est de leurs mesmes invencions. Secondement, pour-

69

tant que toutes les mouches a miel qui sont au monde, ou en Chrestienté, n'ont pas un roy. Tiercement, si toutes les mouches a miel avoient un roy, aussi avons nous, c'est adire Jesus christ. Mais les papistes diront que si nous voulons condamner la papauté, nous condamnerons leurs peres aussy pour hérétiques. Je leur respous ainsi que Dieu respondoit à Eliah : car quand Eliah disoit au Seigneur qu'il n'y avoit pas un qui fust juste, mais que tous e-stoient injustes et mauvais, Dieu re-spondit. Je me suis réservé sept mille

Ephe. 1. D.

3 Rois D. D.
Rom. 11. A.

70

hommes que n'ont point fait obéissance
à Baal : ainsy il ne fault pas douter
qu'il n'y ait eu beaucoup Chrestiens
au monde, desquelz aucuns parloient
a l'encontre de la papauté apertement
et autres gardoient leur sçavoir a eux
mesmes. Mais les papistes ne veulent
pas que nous sachions plus que noz
peres. Je sçay bien que nostre religion ne consiste pas en la vielle coustume et l'usance de noz peres, mais
en la sainte ecriture et parolle divine ;
laquelle (si vous penséz que vieillesse
ct coustume fasse la chose bonne,) est

plus vieille que le monde n'est vieil : Car

Jan. 1. A. Dieu est la parolle, lequel est sans com-
Exod. 3. D. mencement, et sera sans fin ; et si vous
pensez que la vérité doit estre suivie,
toute vérité consiste en ce livre la.
Mais nostre religion ne doit pas estre
gouvernée par noz peres : car Ezechiel
dit, vous ne devéz pas suivre voz peres :
Ezech. 10. E. car ilz estoient mauvais.   Aussy nostre Dieu, sauveur, et rédempteur Jesus
Jan. 14. A. Christ a dit, Je suis la voye, vérité, et vie ;
il n'a pas dit, je suis la vieille coustume.
Les papistes donc disent que combien que Christ n'ordonnast par le pape,

72

qu'il en a laissé faire a son eglise : a donc
je demande comme Pierre estoit esleu
evesque universel ?   Aussy toutes choses
nécessaires à nostre salut sont écrites
en la Bible, comme Paul testifie en son
epistre à Timothée, disant, Tu dois per-   1 Timo. 3. C.
sister aux choses lesquelles te sont com-
mises : pourtant que tu as appris l'écriture, laquelles te donra salut par la foy
en Christ Jesu.

La Seconde Partie.

A quelle intention, donc, voulons nous

prouver que Pierre n'est pas le chef de l'eglise ? prenez le cas qu'il l'ait esté : car cela n'approuve pas que l'evesque de Romme est le chef principal : pourtant que tous les papistes ne pevent pas prouver, que Pierre fust jamais a Romme : car par l'escriture ilz ne le pevent prouver, ny par vraye histoire. Parquoy l'evesque de Romme a perdu un de ses grans tiltres, c'est, Papa ex jure divino. Car nulle authorité ne pœut estre, ex jure divino, si elle n'est approuvée par l'ecriture. Bien maintenant
nous l'avons en un destroit, puis qu'il

est constraint de dire, Paul pape par
les traditions humaines : car s'il n'est
pas evesque par la parolle divine, mais
seulement par les tradicions humaines,
adonc tous rois, tous princes et autres
magistratz pevent abroguer les status
et institucions faites par leurs peres,
comme nous avons veu par cy devant.
Donc si chacun eust congneu cela, le pape eust esté pauvre il y a long
temps. Or les papistes disent que
l'evesque de Romme estoit constitué
par l'eglise primitive ; mais nompas
plus que Mahommet : car ilz commen-

75

çoient tous deux quasi en un mesme temps : mais le pape fut esleu quand toutes mauvaises erreurs estoient grandes en Chrestienté. Toutesfois pour prouver que Pierre estoit à Romme ilz demonstrent les epistres Clementines, lesquelles nous prouverons estre fauses et contrefaites par les papistes : car il est la ecrit que Pierre estoit à Romme en l'an deuxiesme du regne de Claudius, demourant la vint et cinq ans : mais Christ fut crucifié l'an de Tiberius dixhuitiesme, lequel regna cinq ans apres. Caius

Caligula regna quatre ans, et Claudius deux, c'est en tout unze ans devant
que Pierre fust a Romme : Et l'an du
Seigneur dixhuitiesme Paul trouva
Pierre en Jerusalem : parquoy nous   Gal. 2. A.
voyons que leur histoire est fause, et
nous prouverons qu'il n'est pas vray
que Clement ecrivoit les epistres a
Jaques : car Jaques estoit mort devant
l'evesque Clement. Aussy saint Pierre
estoit eveque des Juifz nompas des   Gala. 2. B.
Gentilz : car saint Paul se glorifie, en
beaucoup de places, qu'il est l'Apostre   Eph. 3. A.
des Gentilz. Davantage Paul,

ecrivant aux Galathiens dit qu'il s'en
alloit en Jerusalem acellefin de voir
Pierre : Parquoy il est vray semblable
que Pierre pour la plus part du temps
demouroit a Jerusalem et aux lieux
d'alentour. Mais voyez icy l'astuce
du diable, et le povoir de Dieu : car
ce nonobstant que le diable (acellefin
de confermer son povoir) ait inventé
les epistres Clementines (combien qu'elles
soient contrefaites par les papistes)
toutesfois je dy que Dieu par sa cle-
mence et bonté envers ses esleuz, a
ainsy souffert les epistres estre ecrites,

78

que chacun qui a leu les histoires pœut
facilement comprendre et entendre que
elles estoient feintes par l'astuce serpentine, et par aucuns obstinez et abominables papistes. Aussy nous povons
voir leur astuce en beaucoup d'autres
choses : car quoy que l'ecriture die que
les ydoles n'ont point de vie, ilz faisoient Baruc. 6. A.
que les ymages aucunesfois tournoient
leurs yeux, aucunesfois leur teste, aucunesfois leurs mains, et aucunesfois
tout leur corps : et ainsy faisoient
accroiro aux gens quo les ymages
faites de bois les entendoient, ou toute

la chose estoit faite a viz, lesquelles (en-
tournant) faisoient tourner les yeux
et la teste de l'ymage. Mais comme
Daniel avec dés cendres ou du sablon
L'histoire de prouvoit que l'ydole Bel ne mangeoit
l'ydole Bel. pas, mais que les prestres man-
geoint, ainsi par les saintes ecritures `
et par la confession de plusieurs gens
et notoire expérience, il a esté prouvé
que tout estoit fait a viz et autres in-
strumens.

La Tierce Partie.

Maintenant, puis que nous voyons.

non seulement que Pierre n'est pas le principal, mais aussi qu'il n'estoit pas a Romme (veu qu'ilz disent que le pape ne pœut pas mentir) nous verrons si euxmesmes n'ont pas confessé que nul ne doit estre primat de l'eglise : car Gregoire premier de ce nom ecrivoit que nul ne devoit estre pape : pource qu'alors que Gregoire estoit evesque de Romme et Maurice empereur, il y avoit beaucoup d'heresies en Chrestienté : adonc le patriarche et evesque de Constantinoble prétendoit d'estre evesque universel, auquel Maurice

favorisoit : mais Grégoire ecrivit que
nul ne devoit estre principal de l'eglise.
Maintenant que les papistes sont
vaincus ilz disent que par le consente-
ment des docteurs, et des conciles ge-
neraux, ou doit avoir un evesque universel qui ait nom de pape, la ou quatre ou cinq cens ans apres Christ il
n'y en avoit pas un en tout le monde
qui fust ainsi nommé. Et aussy quand
il y avoit aucunes contencions pour
la papauté, tous les gens sçavans detestoient l'opinion qu'il fausist avoir un
pape : et aucunesfois les evesques de Rom-

me euxmesmes le detestoient. Aussi
Saint Ciprian, écrivant de l'unité de
l'eglise dit, Il y a un evesque dont
chacun evesque tient porcion ; car comme il y a plusieurs rais au soliel, et
la clarté est une : plusieurs branches
et un arbre, plusieurs ruysseaux de-
coulans d'une fontaine, ainsi l'eglise
est une, estant illuminée par la clarté
du Seigneur qui estend ses rais par
tout le monde, et toutesfois la clarté est
une, c'est adire Jesus christ. Pareille-
ment luy estant evesque de Carthage
appelle l'evesque de Romme son com-

Ciprianus de
simplicitate
prelator.

Cipria. epist.
ad Corn.

83

paignon. D'avantage Saint Jerome
evesque de Romme abaisse le stile du

Jeron. Epist.
ad Evag.
primat, disant. S'il est question d'authorité qui sera le primat de l'eglise,
combien qu'il y ait des evesques aux
villes et nations, il ne s'ensuit pas pourtant qu'il y ait un primat de tout le
monde: car le monde est plus grand
qu' une ville. Aussy au concile de Car-

Chap. 47.
thage il fut conclu que nul ne seroit
appellé premier, ou primat des evesques.
Que diray plus? tous consen-

Augustinus
epist. 78 ad
Constan.
tent en un, jusques à six cens ans apres
Christ, que nul ne devoit estre pape.

Comment donc est ce que Pierre povoit estre le primat, ou le pape estre son successeur ? car Pierre en son epistre ne commande pas aux ministres de Dieu, mais les prie. Semblablement quand on l'accuse d'avoir communiqué avec les Gentilz, il ne brule pas ses accuseurs comme le pape fait les siens : mais il se excuse et monstre submission.
D'avantage quand il estoit envoyé en Samarie par ses compagnons, il obeit à leur decret.

August. ad Eulol.

August. 83 ad Aviun. Cipria. Epiat., 76 ad Mauri.

Pierre 1. A.

Actes 11. A.

Actes 8. C.

La Quarte Partie.

De cest abominable et diabolique
pape l'ecriture nous a assez pleinement
demonstré en beaucoup de places, desquelles jé demonstreray aucunes maintenant. Premierement au septiesme
chapitre de Daniel, il est demonstré que
Daniel (le mieux aymé de Balzasar)
vit une vision, laquelle estoit telle, Je
vey dit Daniel en ma vision, et voisy
les quatre vens du ciel combatoient
en la grand mair ; et quatre bestes
sortirent de la terre. La premiere estoit

comme une Lionnesse, et avoit les esles
d'un Aigle et je voyois jusques à ce que
les esles estoient ostées, et le cueur d'un
homme luy fut donné. La seconde
beste estoit semblable à un Ours, et ce   Dan. 7. A.
mettoit dessus un costé : et on luy dit,
mange beaucoup de chair. La tierce
estoit semblable à une Leoparde et avoit
sur son doz quatre esles d'oyseaux : et
ladite beste avoit quatre testes.
Apres je regardois, et voicy la quatriesme beste estoit epouventable, terrible
et forte grandement. Elle avoit grans
dens de fer, et devoroit toutes choses.

Icelle avoit dix cornes : et voicy une pe-
tit corne montoit entre elles, et devoroit trois cornes, et avoit deux yeux
et une bouche, laquelle parloit blasphemes. Mais je regardois jusque a
ce que l'ancien de temps estoit assis.
Apres je regardois, dit Daniel, le jugement de la corne, et la beste estoit
tuée et brulée au feu : Sa vie ne duroit
qu'un temps, deux temps, et demy
temps. Les quatre vens, et les
quatre bestes (comme Melanchton
Œcolampadius, et toutes gens sçavans
disent) signifient les quatre monar-

chies. La premiere estoit des Assirians, où Nabuchodonosor tint l'empire,
auquel (apres avoir este long temps
fait beste) le cueur d'un homme fut
donné. La seconde beste signifioit l'empire des Persans, laquelle estoit tres crue-
lle. La tierce signifioit l'empire des
Grecz, lequel estoit bientost gaigné.
Et les quatre esles et quatre testes signifient les quatre empereurs apres
Alexandre en la Monarchie des Grecz :
car Seleucus fut fait roy de Syrie,
Ptoloméo d'Egipte, Antigone d'Assie,
Cassandre de Grece : La quatriesme

beste signifie la terrible monarchie des
Rommains, hors de laquelle montoit
une petite corne, laquelle est Antichrist.
Antichrist a deux yeux ; c'est adire
le Pape et Mahommet : car combien que
le Pape ne parle pas a l'encontre Christ,
(comme Mahommet fait) toutesfois je
dy que le Pape est aussi bien ou plus
Antichrist que Mahommet. Et comme
celuy qui nous flatte est nostre ennemy (jaçoit ce qu'il semble estre nostre
amy) ainsi le pape que se dit serviteur
des serviteurs de Dieu, est ennemy de
Christ : Pourtant que sous l'umbre

90

de religion, il met en vogue toute ypocrisie, dissimulation, et ydolatrie, avec
toutes autres traditions.   Son temps
sera un temps, deux temps, et un demy temps : c'est adire que les jours seront abbrégéz : car le nombre de sept
est prins pour un nombre parfait en
l'ériture, comme Saint Paul dit ; Le
juste tombe sept fois en un jour, c'esta-
dire, beaucoup de fois.   Et la moytié de
sept, sont trois et demy ; pourtant le
lieu doit estre ainsi entendu, que les   Marc. 13. C.
jours seront abbrégéz.   Saint Paul
aussi en deux epistres prophétise du   2 Thessalo. 2. A.

91

pape. Premierement ecrivant aux
Thessaloniens, il dit, Aussy
mes freres nous vous prions par
l'avenement de nostre Seigneur, que ne
soyéz tost esmeuz en vostre entendement, et que ne soyéz troubléz, ny par
esprit, ny parolle, ny epistre, comme
si la journée de Christ estoit pres.
Que nul ne vous seduise ancunement :
car le jour ne viendra point que premierement ne soit venu un departement, et
que l'homme de peche ne soit revélé, le
filz de perdition, et l'aversaire de Dieu,
et s'eslevera sus tout jusques à estre

assis au temple de Dieu, etc.
Aussy Saint Paul ecrivant à Timothée
dit en ceste maniere, Or l'esprit demon-
stre notamment qu'aux derniers jours   1 Timoth. 4. A.
aucuns defaudront de la foy, s'amu-
sans aux doctrines du diable par l'y-
pocrisie de plusieurs qui parlent men-
songes, defendans mariage,
et manger aucunes choses lesquelles
Dieu a crééées pour en user au fideles avec action de grace. Demandez à un chacun si le pape n'a pas deffendu de manger aucunes viandes en
aucuns temps, et chacun vous dira

93

que ouy ; car la pluspart l'a bien sentu : ou paraventure je ne menterois
pas, si je disois que tous quasi l'ont
bien sentu. Aussy touchant la prohibition de mariage, demandez aux
prestres. Saint Pierre dit, nous sçavons qu'aux derniers jours il viendra
2 Pierre 3. A. des moqueurs, etc. Saint Jan
en l'Apocalipse dit que sept anges jet-
terent sept fiolles d'indignation des-
Apoc. 16. A. sus la terre : pourtant il est vraysem-
blable que la signification est telle.
La premiere fiolle estoit la monarchie
des Assirians, la ou le peuple d'Israel

devint captif souz Nebuchodonosor.
La seconde fiolle estoit la monarchie
des Persans.   La troisiesme fiolle estoit
la monachie des Grecz : laquelle monarchie Alexandre gaigna le premier.
La quarte fiolle estoit la monarchie
des Rommains : laquelle l'Apocalipse
(àcause de sa grandeur) dit qu'elle estoit
jettée sur le soleil.   La cinquiesme est le
pape nostre Antichrist.   La sixiesme
fiolle est le royaume de Mahommet.
La septiesme fiolle signifie la fin du monde et jour du judgement.   Au chapitre
ensuivant il demonstre comme le sept-

95

iesme ange luy demonstra le siege,
honneur, et richesses du pape :
car il dit qu'il voyoit une femme se
Apoc. 17. A. seante sur une beste pleine de noms de
blaspheme, ayant sept testes, et dix cornes.   Ceste femme estoit ornée d'or, et
pourpre, et tenoit une couppe d'or en
sa main pleine des abominations de
la terre : elle avoit ecrit en son front,
La paillarde de Babilone mere des
abominations.   Les sept testes signifient les sept montaignes sur lesquelles
Antichrist demeure : car Romme est
edifiée sur sept montaignes.   Les dix

cornes sont le nombre des rois qui sont
à l'encontre de l'Agneau, lesquelz l'A-
gneau battit et vainquit: car il est le
roy des rois.   Adonc vint l'Ange du
Seigneur disant, Babilone est tombée   Apoc. 18. A.
au feu : ainsi j'ay bon espoir que le royaume d'Antichrist sera destruit : car
combien que les mauvais ayent pros-
périté pour un temps, leur regne ne
sera pas long : mais ceux qui estudient   Deutero.18. A.
la loy du Seigneur, tousjours leur pros-
périté sera longue.   Saint Paul aus-
sy ecrivant a Timothée dit, Or sachez   2 Tim. 3. A.
qu'aux derniers temps, les hommes   2 Pierre 3. A.

97

s'aymeront eux mesmes, et seront ava-
ricieux, vanteurs, orgueilleux, ingratz,
etc.   Isaie le prophete dit que Christ
Isaie. 11. A. battera la terre de la verge de sa bouche, et occira l'homme mauvais par
l'esprit sortant de sa bouche.
Puis donc que nous voyons que le regne d'Antichrist ne demourra pas
pour jamais, il nous fault attendre,
la déstruction de Babilone, et nous
contenter de la voulonté du Seigneur.

Conclusion.

En la premiere partie de nostre livre
nous avons déclaré et prouvé comme

98

Pierre n'estoit pas le primat de l'eglise,
confutans les raisons papistiques.

En la seconde nous avons prouvé qu'ilz
ne pevent alleguer quelque vray tes-
moignage que Pierre ait esté a Romme.
En la troisiesme partie nous avons
prouvé par leurs ditz mesmes qu'ilz
ne dévroient pas avoir la primauté.
En la quatriesme partie nous avons
demonstré les prophesies parlantes de
l'Antichrist. Puis donc que le
Pape est le vray filz du diable, homme
mauvais, un Antichrist, et tiran abominable, prions le seigneur qu'il pré-

serve ceux qui ont veu la lumiere, en
la lumiere : et qu'il monstre a ceux qui
sont en tenebres la vraye, sincere, et pure lumiere : acellefin que tout le monde
en ceste vie glorifie Dieu, et en l'autro
monde soit participant du royaume
eternal par Jesus Christ nostre Seigneur,
auquel avec le pere et la saint esprit,
soit gloire, honneur, empire, et louange
pour tousjamais.   Amen.

Finis.

TRANSLATION.

Edward the Sixth, by the grace of God, King of England, France, and Ireland, Defender of the Faith, and on Earth after God, Head of the Church of England and of Ireland.

To his most dear and well beloved Uncle, Edward Duke of Somerset, Governour of his person, and protector of his Kingdoms, Countries, and Subjects.

After having considered (my dear and well beloved Uncle) how much they displease God who waste all their time on the follies and vanities of this world, spending it in trifling Sports and Diversions, from whence comes no profit or benefit to themselves, or mankind; I have determined to employ myself about the doing something which will be (as I hope) profitable to myself, and acceptable unto you. Having then considered that we see many Papists not only curse us, but call and name us Hereticks, because we have forsaken their Antichrist and its Traditions, and followed the Light which God hath been pleased to afford us; we are inclined to write something to defend us against their contumelies, and lay them (as it is just) upon their own Back. For they call us Hereticks, but Alas! they are so themselves, whilst they forsake the pure voice of the Gospel, and follow their own imaginations, as is most evident from Boniface the Third, who thought (when he was made the universal Bishop) that that falling away which St. Paul speaks of in his second Epistle to the Thessalonians, and second chapter, had happened to him-

self. For Saint Paul saith, We beseech you brethren, by
the coming of our Lord, that ye be not soon shaken in
mind, or be troubled, neither by spirit, nor by word, nor
by letter, as that the day of Christ is at hand. Let no
man deceive you by any means; for that day shall not
come, except there come a falling away first, and that Man
of Sin be revealed, the Son of Perdition; who exalteth
himself above all that is called God, so that he, as God,
sitteth in the temple of GOD, &c.

Notwithstanding he followed his own proud imaginations and fancies, and did not forsake his errors, which
he knew to be very wicked.

Considering then by your life and actions, that you have
a great Affection to the divine word, and the sincere Religion; I dedicate the present work to you praying you to
take it in good part. GOD give you his perpetual grace,
and show his benignity upon you for ever.

From our Palace at Westminster, in London, this last
day of August, 1549.

' A Small Treatise Against the
Primacy of the Pope.

We may easily find and perceive by the experience of
the world, that human nature is disposed to all evils, and
entangled by all manner of vices. For what nation is
there in the earth in which there is not some vice, and
many disorders? And principally in this age because now
there is such an exaltation of the Great Empire of Antichrist:
which is the source of all evil, the fountain of all abomination, and true son of the devil. For when God had sent
his only Son to heal our infirmities, and to reconcile the
world unto himself by his death, the devil instantly
changed the institutions of Christ into human traditions,

and perverted the Holy Scriptures to his purposes and designs, by his minister the Pope. And therefore if the Astrologers (who maintain that all things shall return to their own element) say a truth, the Pope shall descend into hell: for he cannot belong unto God, or be his servant, whilst under the pretence of Religion and the command of God, he usurps unto himself the authority of Christ, as appears in all his works.

Therefore it seemed best to me in this little book, first to condemn the Papacy and afterwards the doctrine of the said Pope. Though I am not ignorant that it is a difficult task, because there are many that will contradict it: notwithstanding we will condemn the Supremacy of the Pope, from the following Reasons.

The First Part.

First then, whereas the papists say, that Rome is the mother of all other churches, and therefore the bishop of Rome ought to be superiour to all other bishops, I answer that it is impossible, because the first promise was made unto the Jews: And Rome was heathen when Jerusalem was Christian; for St. Paul writing to the Romans, says (Rom. xi.) *through their fall, salvation is come unto the Gentiles.* And because the papists cannot prove Rome to have been the mother of all the other churches, they therefore say the bishop of Rome hath received his power from St. Peter: to whom had been given the same Authority with Christ, and remains in the said bishop of Rome to this day, which they endeavour to prove out of these following texts (Mat. xvi.) *Thou art Peter, and upon this Rock I will build my church,* saith Christ, and a little after, *And I will give thee the keys of the Kingdom of Heaven:* And they allege that other place of Scripture, where

Peter says to Christ, *Lord, thou knowest that I love Thee:*
saying that he that loves Christ is the chief, and Peter
loving Christ, more than any of the other apostles loved
him, is therefore the chief and principal of the apostles.
Again, they affirm that he only was commanded to feed
the sheep of Christ, and be the fisher of men, and that he
was the first speaker, and made answer to Jesus (Luke
xxii.), *Behold here are two swords:* from whence the Papists
conclude that Peter had a temporal and a spiritual sword.
They allege also some human reasons, that as the Bees
have one King, so all Christians ought to have one Pope.
And that as there was of old amongst the Jews (Exod. iv.),
a principal priest or bishop (as Moses and Aaron), so now
it is necessary there should be a bishop of the bishops.

Here are two great falsehoods in these few words: the
one is, that the authority and supremacy over the Church
was given to St. Peter; the other that Peter was at Rome.
To the first, where they say that the authority was given
him by these words, Thou art Peter, &c., I answer
that if you remark the preceding and following words
(Mat. xvi.) in that chapter of the Gospel, you will find
that Christ did not speak of Peter, as he was barely a
man, but as he was a believer: for the foregoing words
are, how Peter had said, *Thou art the Son of God:* by
which it is evident that Christ did not say that Peter was
the foundation of the church, but spake of the faith of
Peter. The following words declare how Christ called
Peter satan, but the church of God is not founded upon
satan, therefore it is not founded upon Peter: for if the
church was founded upon St. Peter, it would have a weak
foundation, and, like that house, a sandy foundation that
could not stand long (Mat. vii.) but *the floods came, and
the winds blew, and beat upon that house, and it fell.* In like
manner would the Church fall, if it had so poor a foun-

dation. By which one may see from these words in the text, *Thou art Peter, and upon this stone will I build my church*, must not be understood of Poter, but of the faith of Peter ; upon which the church is founded. For he was a frail and weak vessel, who denied Christ thrice. Their second text is, that the keys of heaven were given to St. Peter (Mat. xvi.). To which I answer that the keys were given not only to Peter, but also to the other apostles. And by this argument I answer that he was not principal, because the rest received the samo authority of the keys that was committed to him. On which account St. Paul calls St. Peter (Gal. ii.) the pillar, not the foundation of the church ; his companion, not his governor. And what are the keys of heaven, the authority of pardoning sin ? No, it is the preaching of the gospel of God the Father, the gospel, I say, of God, not the Pope's or devil's. And as when a door is open, every one who will, may enter therein ; to whom God sent his sincere commandments and gospel, he opened truth, which is the gate of heaven. And he gave unto him an understanding of the Scriptures, which, if they obeyed (2 Cor. ii.) they should thereby be saved. By which we see that the gospel and the truth of the Scriptures are the only gates that conduct men to the kingdom of God. Whence St. Paul says (Rom. x.) *Whosoever shall call upon the name of the Lord shall be saved. How then shall they call on Him in whom they have not believed ? And how shall they believe in Him of whom they have not heard ? And how shall they hear without a preacher ?* And a little after he saith, So then faith cometh by hearing, and hearing by the word of God. And in the fourth chapter to the Romans he also saith (Rom. iv.) *But to him that worketh not, but believeth on him that justifieth the ungodly, his faith is counted for righteousness.* Moreover we will prove that the preaching

of the gospel is the key of heaven. In the eighth chapter
to the Romans, Paul affirms that, *Whoever calls upon the
name of the Lord shall be saved;* and that the preaching of
the gospel is the door that leads to the invocation of the
name of God. Whence it follows, that the preaching of
the gospel is the way and entrance of salvation.

Again, Paul affirms that faith justifies, and that the
preaching of the gospel causes faith (which I have shewn
before) whence it follows that the true preaching of the
Word is the door and entrance to justification. Like as
ground which is sowed may produce fruit, if the seed be
not cast into the ground which is full of thistles, or thorns,
or stones (Mat. xiii., Mark iv., Luke viii.) and yet
although it be sowed on such ground, it will a little
meliorate the earth. So if the word of God be sowed in
the hearts of honest people, or such as have a zeal for
truth, it will confirm them in all goodness; but if any be
obstinate and perverse they cannot impute the fault unto
the Scriptures, that is really in themselves.

Therefore we ought to do our utmost endeavours to
cause the gospel to be preached throughout all the world,
as it is written (Matt. xxviii., Mark xvi., Luke xxiv.)
*All power is given unto Me in heaven and in earth; go
ye therefore, and teach all nations, baptizing them in my
name.*

Since, then, it is proved that the keys of heaven is the
authority of preaching, and that the authority of preaching
was given to all the apostles, I cannot see how, by that
text (Mat. xvi.) any more authority was given to Peter
than to the other disciples. And St. Paul says, he was
not *a whit behind the very chiefest apostles.* Then, if he said
true, St. Peter was not above him. And, if I were asked
which of them was the better, I should say Paul, because
he preached more than them all. But we ought to

account certainly that the Spirit of God was poured out upon them all (Gal. ii., Acts ii.) and that the same spirit of God which filled St. Peter, filled also St. Paul, from whence may be proved that neither of them was superior to the other.

Again, tho Papists say that after Christ was raised from the dead, ho asked (Joh. xxi.) who loved him, and that Peter answered, he loved him, and therefore (say they) he was tho chief apostle. By which reason overy good man ought to have the supremacy over overy other, because each good and pious porson loves God; for it is tho duty and office of overy true Christian. Now tho question is not, whether Peter was faithful, pious, good, a holy and true Christian; but whether he was principal, head, governor, and king above and over tho rest of the apostles and ministers of Jesus Christ? For if the Pope would have the authority of St. Peter, which was to preach, I would be content to give it him; but ho regards but little the precept of God (Joh. vi.) *for Jesus departed into a mountain alone; when he perceived the Jews would make him a king* and emperor. And the Pope, by wrong, or violence, or deceit, hath made all nations subject unto him.

Jesus wore a crown of thorns, and a purple robe was thrown upon Him in derision, and all tho multitude mocked and spit upon Him; but the Pope decks himself with a triple crown, and is adored by kings, princes, emperors, and all estates of porsons. Jesus washed his disciples' feet (Joh. xiii.); and kings kiss the feet of tho Pope. Jesus paid tribute (Mat. xvii.); but the Pope receives, and pays none. Jesus opened his mouth and taught the people (Mat. v.); the Pope takes his case, and rests in his Castle of St. Angelo. Jesus healed all diseases (Luke vi.); the Pope rejoices in blood and

massacres. Christ bore His cross upon His shoulders
(Joh. xix.); the Pope is borne upon the shoulders of men.
Christ came with peace and poverty into the world; the
Pope delights in stirring up war amongst the kings and
princes of the earth. Christ came meekly, humbly, and
compassionately, sitting upon an ass (Mat. xxi.); but the
Pope rides in all pomp and splendour. Christ was a lamb
(Joh. i.); the Pope is a wolf. Christ was poor (Luke ix.);
the Pope would have all christian kingdoms under his
power and command. Christ drove the money-changers
and sellers out of the temple (Joh. ii., Mat. xxi.); the
Pope receives them in. Jesus instituted the sacrament in
commemoration of Himself (Mark xiv., Luke xxii.); tho
Pope formed the mass, a master-piece of imposture. Jesus
ascended into heaven (Mark xvi.); and the Pope falls into
hell. God hath commanded that we should have no other
God but Him (Deut. vi., Exod. xx.); and the Pope makes
himself to be honoured like unto a great god. God forbids
us to commit idolatry (Mat. iv.); and the Pope is the
author of image worship. God hath prohibited swearing
in vain (Exod. xx.) but the Pope allows his friends per-
jury. God hath commanded the use of festivals in good
works, prayers, and devotions; but the Pope allows pomp,
games, idleness, mimicry to be exercised on those days in
churches. God hath forbidden murder, and killing any
person; and it is a matter of great compassion and sorrow
to see how cruelly the Pope persecutes Christians. God
foretold this persecution in the four-and-twentieth chapter
of Matthew (Mat. xxiv.) *Many false prophets, says Christ,
shall arise at that time; and because iniquity shall abound, the
love of many shall wax cold; but the gospel shall be preached in
all the world; when ye therefore shall see the abomination
of desolation, spoken of by Daniel the prophet, stand in the
holy place, then let them which be in Judea flee into the mountains.*

And is not this come to pass now? Yea, for there are many wolves in sheep's clothing, who, under the pretence of religion, obscure the true doctrine of Christ; and almost all abominations were introduced into the holy place, that is to say, brought into the church of God.

But to return to our matter, God hath forbidden adultery; notwithstanding the Pope, who will be obedient to his father the Devil, commands his priests to keep concubines and harlots, rather than give themselves to any in marriage. God hath forbidden stealing from either man, woman, or child; but the Pope is such an old thief that he robs even God of his honour, and transfers it to himself. God hath forbidden bearing false witness against any one; but the Pope cries all is good grist which comes to his mill. God hath commanded us to be content with what is our own, but the Pope will have every house pay him a tribute. To conclude, he is in every thing opposite to God. But I cannot blame him, for he fulfils the command of Paul, which says (Eph. vi.), *Children obey your parents:* and the Demon of hypocrisy is his father, to whom he pays all obedience. *The Devil walketh about as a roaring lion* (saith St. Peter) *seeking whom he may devour* (1 Pet. v.). And does not the Pope do the same? Yes, certainly, for he not only ordains wicked and unjust laws, but he pursues to death all who have a true zeal and love towards God.

But to return to the primacy of Peter. I ask how many kingdoms St. Peter had under his dominion? For it was impossible that all kingdoms should be under him, when St. James was then bishop of Jerusalem, and that city then christian. Neither can I see how Peter should be the chief. For St. Paul says to the Corinthians, concerning the Apostles (1 Cor. viii.), *All are yours, and you are*

Christ's, and Christ is God's. Likewise St. Peter calls himself by no other title (1 Pet. i.), but *Peter, an apostle of Jesus Christ,* by which it is manifest, that we are not Peter's, but Peter ours. Again, when Paul came to Antioch *he withstood Peter to his face, because he was to be blamed* (Gal. ii.): which he would not have done if Peter had any such authority, or could not have lyed, as they say: but (as I have said thereupon) Paul, seeing the dissimulation of Peter, said unto him, *If thou, being a Jew, livest after the manner of the Gentiles, and not as do the Jews, why compellest thou the Gentiles to live as do the Jews? We, who are Jews by nature, and not sinners of the Gentiles, knowing that a man is not justified by the works of the law, but by the faith of Jesus Christ, even we have believed in Jesus Christ, that we might be justified by the faith of Christ, and not by the works of the law,* &c. Let us then see how it is possible that Peter should be chief; for if he was principal, who loved Christ the best, it is evident that St. John would be the chief of the Apostles, for Christ appointed him to take care of his Mother, and John lay in the bosom of Jesus, whilst he supped (Joh. xix.; Joh. xiii.). But to the matter in hand, I ask, Whether a lawful council can be called but by the Pope? to which I am sure the papists will answer negatively. Then I ask if the Pope can call a council before his election, to which I know they will reply he cannot. If, then, no Council is lawful without a Pope, and that none who is labouring to be elected Pope can assemble a Council, then the Council which confirms the Pope superior over the Church is not lawful, because it was not convocated by a Pope, being there was then none elected. But being thus driven from the argument, they fly to another, and say that Christ commanded Peter to feed his sheep (Joh. xxi.); but he commanded all the rest to do the same (Mat. xxviii.), saying, *Go ye therefore and teach all nations, baptizing them in My name.* But the Pope does not obey the commandment of Jesus Christ. For he doth not feed his sheep, but devours them like a roaring lion (1 Pet. v.), who walks about to seek his prey. Now I wish the Pope would obey the commandment of God which he gave to St. Peter: for I should not regret his having authority to preach Christ to all the world, but he leaves the preaching of the gospel and usurps the authority of being head of the church, which of right belongs to none but Christ. 'Tis true the Pope is primate of the church, but 'tis not the divine or Catholick Church, but the diabolical one. For he transgresses the commandment given in general to St. Peter and the rest of the Apostles. For when Christ sent his twelve Disciples to preach the gospel of repentance and the kingdom of God, he said (Mat. x.), *Behold, I send you forth as sheep among wolves.* But the bishop of Rome is like a wolf among sheep, eating and devouring the poor sheep of Christ, and when they are hid by fear he takes the voice of the sheep to betray and devour them. He excuses himself from preaching upon its being too low and mean an office for him, saying he hath lower officers and ministers for that work, whilst he is taken up with seeing and attending to the singing out of the masses. But I answer to the first, that if the office of preaching was not below St. Peter, who had received all his authority and power from Christ himself, methinks that those who call themselves the successors of Peter, should not esteem the office too mean for them.

St. Paul writes to Timothy what every Bishop ought to be (1 Tim. iii.): *A Bishop* (saith he) *must be blameless, the husband of one wife, sober, of good behaviour, given to hospitality, apt to teach, not given to wine, no striker, not given to filthy lucre, but one that ruleth well his own house, having his children in subjection with all gravity.* Now let us arraign

the Pope before St. Paul, and examine whether by St.
Paul's rule he be guilty or not. The first commandment
to a bishop is to be blameless; but we have proved that
the bishop of Rome transgresses all the commandments of
God, by which he stands guilty. The second is, that he be
the husband of one wife, in which the bishop of Rome
errs mightily; for he allows concubines, and counts filthy
fornication better than lawful and honest marriage. The
third is that he should be sober, and full of wisdom and
virtue, which the bishop of Rome very little observes.
The fourth is that he be liberal, given to hospitality,
not greedy of filthy lucre; but the bishop of Rome is
full of avarice and oppression. The fifth is that he be
apt to teach, but our devil or diabolical father accounts
maintaining the glory of God by preaching, is too mean
an office for him, notwithstanding his predecessor Peter,
either preached the gospel, or sinned against God in not
observing that commandment (Mat. xxviii.), Go ye and
preach the gospel over all the world. But he will im-
prison, slay, and burn those who do preach the word,
and would himself be their executioner if he did not find
others to do it in his stead, by which we may see that
he loves himself more than he loves God. What shall I
say more? He disobeys all the orders of St. Paul, give
verdict therefore whether he be guilty or innocent.

But now we will proceed to their other arguments, and
first to their maintaining Peter to be the chief, for which
they allege his being commanded to feed the sheep (Joh.
xxi.). To which I answer that all the Apostles were commanded as well as he to feed the sheep of Christ, in
these words of the Gospel (Mat. xxviii.), *Go ye all and preach,*
&c. For the preaching of the Gospel signifies nothing
else but feeding the sheep. And their other argument is
not more substantial, when they say, Peter was a fisher of

men: for I say, Andrew and John were by the same authority made fishers of men; for fishers of men are really nothing but preachers of Christ.

Now if the preaching of the gospel be unlawful, without authority from Peter the Pope; then the preaching of St. Paul was not lawful, because he did not receive the authority from Peter; notwithstanding the pope accounts himself a God, saying, I cannot lie, therefore I have spoken truth. To which I answer, that if he be not greater than Peter, he may lie; for Peter denied Christ thrice (Mat. xxvi.), Peter then lied thrice; and St. Paul afterwards reproved him for his dissimulation (Gal. ii.). But the bishop of Rome lies notoriously, if in nothing else, but in his pretending to be the head of the Christian Church, and having the keys of heaven. For if the pope have the keys of heaven, make this query: when the pope is dead, and none hath the keys, how can any soul enter into heaven? No person till he be elected pope having the keys: whence it must follow, that the pope being dead, heaven's gates are closed. But it is a folly to say that the pope hath the keys of heaven and hell, when Christ is our only mediator (1 Tim. ii.), our gate, Head, Shepherd, Redeemer, and sovereign Lord; who (after he had taught, instructed, done many miracles, and suffered death for us (Matt. xxvii.), and pronounced salvation to all that believe on his name (Mark xvi.; Luke xxiv.; Joh. xix.; Mat. xxviii.), and from the power of his passion faithfully believes to be saved) ascended into heaven with great honour and glory, and is seated on the right hand of God his father, where he intercedes for us; remaining for ever with his blessed father and the Holy Ghost, one God in Trinity, and three persons in Unity, full of power and virtue, and free from vice and sin; remaining with us by his spirit, and being in every respect equal with his father,

till he shall come in glory to be judge of all the world
(Eph. i.; Heb. i., iv.; Matt. xxv.), whose greatness is in-
scrutable, mercy unexpressible, and glory most ines-
timable; He is our Governor and Master; He is our
Shepherd and Redeemer, and we are his subjects and
sheep (Psal. xxii.); we are ransomed by his blood, and
washed by the waters of baptism to show that we are his
sheep (Joh. x.); none else is our pastor or Lord: neither
the pope nor any on earth can be our Lord; else we
should become a monster having two heads. Paul, writing
to the Corinthians, says (1 Cor. iii.), that all is ours; Peter,
Apollos, and all the other apostles were ours, and we are
Christ's, and Christ is God's; whereby it appears that
Peter is not a head but a minister unto us. Therefore we
must esteem God our spiritual father, who by the passion
of Christ, took from us all the pains of death and hell, to
all who believe in him; that is the spirit of adoption
whereby we cry *Abba*, Father (Rom. viii.). If the pope then
will be called our spiritual father, we shall have three fathers,
whereof the one is carnal, and two spiritual, neither can
the pope be so, for as Christ is the immaculate lamb, and
only son of God, endued with all power: on the other
side, the pope is an unclean and ravenous wolf, and only
son of the devil his father, from whom he hath received
his authority and office.

But I would fain know whether the pope be our spiritual,
carnal, or diabolical father. In the first place. I cannot
allow he can be our carnal father, because he lives celibate,
and makes a profession of chastity: neither can he be our
spiritual father, being so addicted to the world, and
worldliness; then it follows that he must be our diabolical
father. Let us, therefore, conclude, that it was said of
Christ, *Thou art my son, this day have I begotten thee* (Psal.
2); God will say to the pope, Thou art my enemy, this

day have I destroyed thee: and as Christ was of the order
of Melchisedek (Psalm cx.), so the pope is of the order
diabolic. But as Christianity is spiritually very good,
and well designed; yet if there be not good order to
preserve it, it must decay. As the body of a man could
not be healthy with two heads, four arms, or four feet; so
these Christian countries could never well subsist under
the distraction of two equal sovereigns. But some may
question me then, and say, What then, you would not
have any kings or emperors? But to that I answer, that
God who sent his only son down into the world, made him
king over it (Mat. i.), putting all spiritual and temporal
authority into his hands (Psalm cx.); he by his sove-
reignty hath placed kings to be his lieutenants over the
earth; but he hath not ordained any supreme bishop, for
we find none so authorised by the Holy Scripture. Now
if the papists say that the pope is heir to him, I would
advise him then, to stay till Christ were dead before they
seized upon his kingdom: because no heirs take the possession of their inheritances till after the death of their
predecessors.

Moreover, the papists say, that as under the old law
(Exod. iv.) there was a high priest, or archbishop of the
Jews; so there ought now to be a head or supreme
minister amongst christians. To which I answer, that
the priesthood of Aaron and Moses represented the supremacy of our Saviour Christ, not the Pope. For Christ
who came down to the earth (Mat. i.) and suffered death
for us, says of himself, that he was our Messias (John iv.),
and that he was the true bread which came down from
heaven (John vi.), and our only shepherd; for St. John
testifies that he says (John x.), *I am the door: he that
entereth not by me into the sheepfold, but climbeth some other
way, is a thief; but he that entereth in by the door is the Shep-*

herd of the sheep. To him the porter openeth, and the sheep hear his voice: And he calleth his own sheep by name, and leadeth them out, and the sheep follow him, for they know his voice; and a stranger will they not follow. But the pope not coming by Christ is an abominable thief: therefore all true and good sheep ought to fly from him: for he comes to devour, not to feed them; to prey upon them, not to instruct them. But the papists, being thus scourged with their own rod (to wit, with their own argument) say farther, that after the disciples had preached about the cities, after they returned to Jesus, he asked them: Whether they had any sword with them? and that they answered, Here are two swords. Now they urge farther, that the one of the swords signifies the spiritual, the other the temporal power: which reason (as shall be shewn hereafter) is selfish and vain. For first, we ought to consider from whence the apostles came; they had been sent (Mark vi.) *to preach Christ to all people,* and (Luke ix.) *to shew the light to those that sat in darkness.* Secondly, we must consider the power Christ had on earth, for he said himself, that his kingdom was not of this world; and there are two sorts of authority, the one spiritual and the other temporal. On which account St. Paul writes in his first epistle to the Corinthians (1 Cor. xii.) *as the body is one, and hath many members,* for several uses, so there are also in the church of Christ, amongst the spiritual ministers; first, apostles; secondarily, prophets; thirdly, teachers; and some temporal ministers, as kings, emperors, governors, and lieutenants. Now Christ was a spiritual minister, as he testifies of himself, saying, *My kingdom is not of this world.* And again, when two brethren came unto him and requested him to divide their inheritance between them, he answered (Luke xii.), *Man, who made me a judge or divider over you?* The third thing to be considered is, that Christ

spake to the disciples concerning the swords ironically.
Fourthly, that all the apostles answered together, Behold
here are two swords. Fifthly, you may observe in the text,
that the apostles understood not what Christ meant.

By all which things we may easily understand that text;
for after the apostles had been sent to preach the gospel of
truth, when they returned to Jesus, he said unto them,
Had you any sword with you then? (as much as to say),
When I sent you first out, you would have staves with you,
but now what do you think, hath not my grace kept you
from all evil? or else, what need have you had of a sword?
Then his disciples (not Peter only), understanding not what
Christ said, answered, there were two swords.

By which we see Christ spoke ironically, and that all his
disciples made answer, not Peter alone; as if he should
say, I have two swords, the one signifying my temporal
authority, and the other signifying the spiritual jurisdic-
tion; neither would nor could Christ give a temporal
authority, forasmuch as he was a spiritual minister.
And the Papists err extremely in one argument, where
they say, that Cephas is a head, whereas in truth Cephas
is a stone; (but when these their arguments were weakened)
then they cry it is probable, that Peter was the chief
apostle, because he spake first at that time concerning our
dispute, and so answered in behalf of all the Apostles.

But it is more likely he was not the prince over the rest,
because St. Paul says (1 Cor. xi.) *For I suppose I was not
a whit behind the very chiefest apostles; for in nothing I am
behind the very chiefest apostles* (2 Cor. xii.) In which
number Peter is comprised. Now we must not dispute
what is most probably true, but what is most certainly
true. Nevertheless, let us examine whether it be probable
or not: for Andrew sometimes spake first, and it is not to
be doubted but that each of them sometimes spake first;

but it does not therefore follow that he who speaks sometimes first, must be bishop of the bishops : his first speaking at that time may signify that he was of a very courage-
ous spirit; or else that he could have desired to have been
the greatest : But Christ said (Matt. xviii. ; Luke i.) *They
that humble themselves like a little child shall be the greatest
in the kingdom of heaven ;* neither is there any lofty, proud
title, in the kingdom or church of Christ, as you may see
in that magnificate in Luke, for God loves humility
(Rom. xii. ; Phil. ii.); and Christ says (Luke ix.) in Luke,
*If any man desire to be first, the same shall be the last of all
and servant unto all.* And in another evangelist, he saith
(Matt. xviii.) *Whoso receiveth one such little child in my name
receiveth me ; and unless ye become as little children, ye shall
not be fit for the kingdom of heaven.* Nor does Peter attri-
bute so high a title to himself, as the Pope takes upon
him. For he writes thus in his epistle (2 Pet. i.), *Peter, a
servant and an apostle of Jesus Christ,* and no more. But
the Pope—what does he say? *Paul the third by the grace
of God, the most Holy Pope and Father, Deputy to Peter, and
Vicar to Christ, King of Kings, Prince of Princes, Bishop
of the Bishops, and God on earth.* Behold, therefore, how
he calls himself God, and blasphemes Christ. Behold
how he is filled and puffed up with pride and vanity.
Behold how large and fair a name and title he takes,
though he be a venomous serpent, calling himself the most
holy father, whereas he is a detestable thief, and con-
taminated with all uncleanness. He calls himself the
pope, which word signifies father unto all nations, whilst
he brings them to destruction. Nay, he calls himself the
vicar of Christ, and deputy of St. Peter, and god upon
earth ; whilst he is vicar to Beolzebub, deputy to Lucifer,
and a terrestrial demon ; for he would seem to be very
good, whilst he is very wicked. And it is no wonder if

the ministers of the devil appear brave and triumphant outwardly, for St. Paul writes to the Corinthians (2 Cor. ii.), *No marvel what false apostles, and deceitful workers can transform themselves into; Satan himself being transformed into an angel of light.*　　•

Wherefore you may easily discern the true ministers of the word from the false antichrists; because the true apostles walk after the spirit of God, and the false walk after the flesh. Let us, therefore, see whether the Pope be the minister of God, or of the devil; which I fear he will prove; proclaiming himself a good man, a most holy bishop, a king of kings; whereas he is the tyrant of tyrants; for all others exercise their tyranny over bodies, but this devil, wolf, tyrant, exercises his over the souls of men, constraining the poor and simple lambs of God to forsake their faith, whereby they are saved, to follow his abominable traditions and diabolical precepts. Which if they refuse to obey, to wit, adoring images, and offering to his idols and devils, he burns, racks, and torments them, or forces them to a costly recantation.

During the reign of my late father the king, when the pope's name was blotted out of our books, he stopped the mouths of christians with his Six Articles, as if he would choke them.

And at this day in France, before any one is burnt, a little before the execution, they cut out his tongue, that they might not speak. Considering then that the Pope is the minister of Lucifer, I am in good hopes, that as Lucifer fell from heaven into hell, so the pope, his vicar, will fall from the great glory of the papacy into contemptible derision. For David hath said (Ps. xviii.) in the Psalms, *With the pure thou wilt shew thyself pure, and with the froward thou wilt shew thyself froward.* Again, the Pope hath taken God's honour away from him, therefore I hope

God will divest him of his honours and glory. As Mary the mother of Jesus saith (Luke i.), *He hath put down the mighty from their seats, and exalted them of low degree.* Take heed of thyself, then, O Pope, for if thou tumblest thou wilt have a terrible fall. As a man who has got up into a high tower would have a huge leap if he should fall down, so thou who hast exalted thyself unto the heavens, would fall down unto the abyss of hell, as Christ foretold of Tyre and Sidon (Matt. xi.).

But to return to the pope's primacy. I know very well that the Scripture speaks of one God, one faith, one baptism (Eph. iv.; 1 Cor. viii.; 1 Tim. ii.; Matt. xix.), but no mention of one Pope. Now if Peter had been a god on earth, and vicar of Christ, we should have been baptized into his name. But (2 Cor. xi.; 2 Cor. xii.) Paul (who affirms himself to be inferior to none of the other apostles) will not allow us to be baptized into his name; nay he is so far from having us baptised into the name of Peter, that he will not have it said, I am of Peter, or of Paul, or of Apollos.

And now that the papists cannot prove by the Scriptures that we ought to have one pope, they run to similitudes, saying, that as the creatures in the earth (as the bees) have a king over them, so all Christians ought to have one king and pope. To which I will answer three ways. First, that their reason is not extracted from the Holy Scripture, but from their own invention. Secondly, that all the bees which are in the world, or in Christendom, have not one king. Thirdly, that if all bees have their king; so have we, to wit, Jesus Christ (Eph. i.).

But the papists will then say, that if we condemn the papacy, we shall condemn our forefathers as heretics. I will answer to that, as God answered Elijah (1 Kin. xix.) when he said to the Lord, that the children of Israel had forsaken his covenant, and were unjust and wicked, *yet I have left me seven thousand in Israel, all the knees which have not bowed to Baal.* Neither must we imagine, but that there have been many Christians in the world, some of which have spoken openly against the papacy, and others that have kept their knowledge and sentiments to themselves; but the papists will not suffer us to know more than our fathers. But I know very well, that our religion consists not of old customs, or the usage of our fathers; but in the Holy Scriptures, and Divine word. And that (if you think antiquity and custom makes a thing good) is older than the world. For God is the Word, who was without beginning (Joh. i.), and shall continue without end (Exod. ii.), and if you think truth ought to be followed and obeyed, all truth is contained in that book. Our religion ought not to be steered or governed by our forefathers: for Ezechiel saith (Ezech. xx.) *Walk ye not in the statutes of your fathers, for they were polluted.* Moreover, our God and Saviour, and Redeemer, Jesus Christ said (John xiv.), *I am the way, and the truth, and the life:* he did not say, I am the old custom.

The papists then say, that though Christ did not indeed ordain the pope, yet he left it to the church to do it. To which I ask, how Peter then was elected the universal bishop? For all things necessary to our salvation are written in the Bible; as St. Paul testifies (1 Tim. iii.) in his Epistle to Timothy, where he says, *But continue thou in the things which thou hast learned, &c. And that from a child thou hast known the Holy Scriptures, which are able to make thee wise unto salvation, through faith which is in Christ Jesus.*

The Second Part.

But to what purpose do we go about to prove that Peter

is not the head of the Church? For allow he had been so, that does not conclude that the bishop of Rome is the principal head. For the papists themselves cannot prove that Peter was ever at Rome, because by the Scripture they cannot prove it; nor by any true history. Therefore the bishop of Rome loses one of his great titles, of *Papa ex jure Divino*, for no authority can be *ex jure Divino*, unless it be confirmed by the Scripture. Well, then, we have him in a great plunge, since he must be forced to say, Paul, pope by human traditions; for if he be not bishop by the divine word, but only by human traditions then all kings, princes, and other magistrates, may abrogate the statutes and institutions made by their fathers, as we have seen before. If every one then had known this, the pope had been poor long ago. Now the papists say, that the bishop of Rome was instituted by the primitive church; but no more than Mahomet, for they begun near the same age, and the pope was elected when all manner of wicked errors were advanced in Christendom.

Nevertheless to prove that Peter was at Rome, they produce the Clementine Epistles; but we will prove them counterfeited, and falsified by the Papists. For in them it is written that Peter was at Rome, in the second year of the reign of Claudius, and lived there twenty-five years; but Christ was crucified in the eighteenth year of Tiberius, and he reigned five years after the Crucifixion. Caius Caligula reigned four years, and Claudius two, which makes it eleven years before Peter went to Rome. And in the eighteenth year of our Lord, Paul found St. Peter in Jerusalem (Gal. i.); by which we see their history is false. And we will prove that it is not true that Clement wrote these epistles unto James, for James was dead before Clement was bishop. Moreover, St. Peter was the bishop of the Jews, and not of the Gentiles (Gal. ii):

for St. Paul glories in several places that he was the
Apostle of the Gentiles. Again St. Paul writing to the
Galatians says (Gal. i.) that he went up to Jerusalem to
see Peter; therefore it is most probable, that Peter dwelt
for the most part in Jerusalem, or in the adjacent cities.
And here we may see the craft of the devil and the power
of God; for notwithstanding the devil (to establish his
power) invented the Clementine Epistles (though they be
counterfeited by the papists); yet I say, God by his goodness and clemency towards his elect, hath caused the said
epistles to be so written, that every one who hath read
history, may plainly comprehend and understand, that
they were feigned by serpentine subtilty, and by some
abominable and obdurate papists.

In several other instances also, we may discover their
false subtilty; for notwithstanding that the Holy Scripture
saith, idols are senseless things and without life, they
have often framed images which sometimes rolled their
eyes, sometimes turned their heads, sometimes moved their
hands, and sometimes their whole bodies; by which means
they made people believe, that an image made of wood,
heard and understood them; all of it being made so to
the life, that (as they turned them) they made the head
and eyes of the image to turn also. But as Daniel with
ashes or sand, proved the idol Bel did not eat, but his
priests; so by the Holy Scriptures, the confession of
several persons, and by observation and experience, they
have been proved to have been mere machines, and other
instruments.

The Third Part.

Since we see that Peter neither was the chief, nor was
at Rome (considering that they say the Pope cannot lie),

we will examine whether they themselves have not acknowledged that no person ought to be the primate of the Church.

For Gregory the first hath written, that none ought to be Pope. Gregory was then bishop of Rome, and Maurice was emperor, and there were many heretics in Christendom; and the bishop and patriarch of Constantinople, at that time pretended to be the universal bishop, who was much favoured by Maurice. But Gregory declared then in his writings, that there ought to be no principal in the Church.

And now the papists are overthrown by this: they say that by the consent of the General Councils, and doctors, an universal bishop was established under the name of pope: whereas for four or five hundred years after.Christ, there was no person in the world that was distinguished or called by that name. Moreover, when there were several contentions about the papacy, all learned persons detested the opinion that there must be a pope: and sometimes the very bishops of Rome themselves abhorred it. And St. Cyprian,* writing concerning the unity of the Church, saith, There is one bishop, of whom every bishop holds a share. For as there are many beams in the sun, yet the brightness is but one: many branches in a tree: several streams from a fountain; in like manner, the Church is but one, which being illuminated by the brightness of our Lord, who extends his beams throughout all the world, yet nevertheless the clarity is but one, to wit, Jesus Christ. Likewise the same Cyprian,† being bishop of Carthage, calls the bishop of Rome his companion. Moreover St. Jerome,‡ bishop of Rome, humbles the style of primate, saying, if there be any question of

* Cyprian, *De Simplicitate Prelatorum.*
† Cyprian, *Epist. ad Corn.*   ‡ Jerom, *Epist. ad Evag.*

the authority of a primate of the church, although there are bishops of nations and cities, it follows not therefore that there is a primate over all the world, for the world is much greater than any city. And also in the Council of Carthage it was decreed, that none should be called the first or primate of the bishops. What shall I say more? It was consented and agreed by all,* for six hundred years after Christ, that none ought to be Pope. How could Peter then have been primate, or the Pope his successor? For Peter in his Epistles does not command, but pray and beseech the ministers of God. Likewise when he is accused for having communicated with the Gentiles (Acts xi.), he does not burn his accusers, as the Pope does his: but excuses himself, and shews a submission.

Again, when he was sent to Samaria by his brethren and companions (Acts viii.) he readily obeyed their decree and went down to that City.

The Fourth Part.

Of this detestable and diabolical pope, the holy Scriptures in several places give us a plenary demonstration; some of which I shall shew unto you. As first, in the fourth of Daniel, it is set down how that Daniel (that was beloved by Belshazzar) saw a vision, which appeared to him thus: *I saw, says Daniel, in my vision by night, and behold the four winds of heaven strove upon the great sea, and four great beasts came up out of the earth: the first was like a lion, and had eagle's wings: and I beheld till the wings thereof were plucked, and a man's heart was given to it. The second beast was like unto a bear, and it raised up itself on one side; and they said thus unto it, Arise, devour much flesh. The third was like unto a leopard, which had upon the back of it four wings of a fowl, and*

* August. Ep. 28 ad Const.

*the said beast had also four heads. After this I beheld the
fourth beast, which was dreadful and terrible, and strong ex-
ceedingly; and it had great iron teeth; and devoured every-
thing; and it had ten horns. And behold, there came up
among them another little horn, before whom there were three of
the first horns plucked up by the roots; and it had eyes, and a
mouth, speaking blasphemies. And I beheld till I saw the
Ancient of Days did sit, and I beheld, saith Daniel, till the
judgment was set for the horn, and till the beast was slain, and
his body given to the burning flame: and it shall be for a
time, times, and a half.* Now the four winds and the four
beasts (as Melancthon, Œcolampadius, and all the learned
writers say) signify the four monarchies; the first was that
of the Assyrians, whereof Nebuchadnezzar was emperor;
who (after he had been made like unto the beasts for a
long season) had the understanding of a man given him
again. The second signified the empire of the Persians,
which was a dominion of great cruelty. The third notified
the Grecian Empire, which was immediately raised to its
grandeur; and the four wings, and four heads signify the
four emperors, who succeeded Alexander, and divided
among them the Grecian monarchy.

For Seleucus was made king of Syria, Ptolemy got
Egypt, Antigonus Asia, and Cassander Greece. The
fourth beast signifies the terrible monarchy of the
Romans, out of which arises a little horn, which is Antichrist; and Antichrist hath two eyes, viz., the pope and
Mahomet; for notwithstanding that the pope doth not
speak against Christ (as Mahomet doth), nevertheless I
answer that the pope is as much, or rather more
an Antichrist than Mahomet. For as he who
flatters us is our enemy (though he seems to be our
friend), so the pope, who styles himself the servant of
the servants of God, is the enemy of Christ; whilst

under the shadow of religion, he puts in practico all hypocrisy, idolatry, dissimulation, and all sorts of traditions; his time shall be a timo, times, and a half; that is to say, his days shall be shortened. For the number seven stands for a perfect number in Scripture; for St. Paul says, the just fall seven times a day; to wit, often. Now the half of seven is three and-a-half; thorefore we must interpret by that imperfect time, that those days shall bo shortened. St. Paul also in two Epistles prophesies of tho popo. First, writing to the Thessalonians, ho says (2 Thess. ii.), *Now we beseech you brethren, by the coming of our Lord, that ye be not soon shaken in mind or be troubled, neither by spirit nor by word nor by letter, as that the day of Christ is at hand. Let no man deceive you by any means, for that day shall not come, except there come a falling away first, and that man of sin be revealed, the Son of Perdition; who opposeth and exalteth himself above God, so that he as God sitteth in the temple of God,* &c. Again, St. Paul, writing to Timothy (1 Tim. iv.) speaks thus: *Now the spirit speaketh expressly that in the latter times some shall depart from the faith, giving heed to doctrines of devils, speaking lies in hypocrisy, forbidding to marry, and commanding to abstain from meats, which God hath created to be received with thanksgiving of them which believe.*

Now let every one bo asked if tho Popo hath not forbidden certain meats at certain times, and they must all confess he hath, for most folks have felt it; or perchance I should not bo a liar if I said that almost all folks havo. And concerning tho prohibition of marriage, ask their own priests. St. Petor tells us that thero shall come in the last days, scoffers, &c. (2 Pet. iii.). St. John, in tho Apocalypse, says (Apo. xvi.): Seven angels poured out the vials of God's wrath upon tho earth: and the signification is probable to bo thus. Tho first vial to bo the Assyrian Monarchy, when the people of Israel became captive to Nebuchadnezzar. The second the Persian Monarchy. The third the Monarchy of the Grecians, which Alexander first established. The fourth was the Roman Monarchy, which the Apocalypse (because of its grandeur) says, the fourth vial was poured upon the sun. The fifth is our Antichrist, the pope. The sixth vial is the dominion of Mahomet. The seventh vial signifies the end of the world, and the day of judgment.

In the following chapter he declares that one of the Seven Angels came and talked with him, and showed him the state, honour, and riches of the pope; for he says, (Apo. xvii.) he saw *A woman sit upon the beast, full of names of blasphemy, having seven heads and ten horns; and the woman was arrayed in purple and scarlet colour, and decked with gold, having a golden cup in her hand, full of abominations and filthiness of her fornications; and upon her forehead was written, Babylon, the mother of harlots, and abominations of the earth.* The seven heads signify the seven hills which Antichrist dwells on (Apo. xvii.) for Rome is built upon seven mountains. The ten horns are the number of the kings who made war with the lamb, and the lamb overcame them, for he is Lord of Lords, and King of Kings. Then another angel came down from heaven (Apo. xviii.) crying, *Babylon is fallen, and is become the habitation of devils;* thence I hope that the kingdom of Antichrist shall be destroyed. For, though the wicked may prosper for a time, their dominion shall not last; but those who study the law of the Lord, their prosperity shall last for ever. St. Paul, writing to Timothy (1 Tim. iii.) says, This know also, that in the last days, men shall be lovers of their own selves, covetous, boasters, proud, blasphemers, &c. And the prophet Isaiah saith (Isa. xi.) that Christ *shall smite the earth with the rod of his mouth, and with the breath of his lips shall he slay the wicked.*

Since we see, then, that the reign of Antichrist shall not last for ever, we must wait for the destruction of Babylon, and submit ourselves to the will of the Lord.

The Conclusion.

In the first part of our book, we have proved and declared that Peter was not primate of the Church, by confuting all the papistical reasons for it.

In the second, we have proved that they cannot produce and allege any true testimony that St. Peter was at Rome.

In the third part we have proved from themselves that they have said they ought not to have the primacy.

In the fourth part, we have explained the prophecies speaking of Antichrist. Since, then, the pope is that wicked one—very son of the devil, an Antichrist, and an abominable tyrant; let us pray unto the Lord to preserve those still in the light who have seen it, and that He will show the sincere, pure, and true light unto those who sit in darkness; that all the world may glorify God in this life, and be partakers of the eternal Kingdom of Heaven in the world to come, by the merits of Jesus Christ our Saviour; to whom with the Father, and the Holy Ghost, be all honour, glory, dominion, and praise, for ever and ever. Amen.

DISCOURSE
ON THE REFORMATION OF ABUSES.
1551.

DISCOURSE.

The governaunce of this realme is devided into tow partes on[e] ecclesiasticall, th' other temporell.

Th' ecclesiasticall consisteth in settingforth the worde of God, continewing the peple in prayer, and the discipline. The settingfurth of the worde of God consisteth in the good discreet doctrine and example of the teachours and spirituall officers. For as the good husbandmane maketh his ground good and plentifull, so doth the true preachour with doctrine and example print and grafe ou the peple's mind the word of God, that they at lenghte become plentifull. Wherefore Prayers to God also must be made continually of the peple, and officers of the Church to assist them with his grace. And thos prayers must first with good consideracion be setfurth, and fantes therin be amendid; next being setfurth the peple must continually be allured to heire them. For discipline, it were very good that it wentfurth, and that those that did notablye offend in swearing, rioting, neglecting of God's word, or such like vices, were duely punished, so that thos that shuld be th' execntours of this discipline were men of tried honesty, wisdom, and judgment. But bicause thos bishops whoe shuld execute, some for papistrye, some for ignoraunce, some for age, some for their ill name, some for al theis, ar[e] men unable to execute discipline, it is therofor a thing unmete for thies men. Wherefore it were necessary that those that were apointed to be bishops or preachours were honest in life and lerned in their doc-

trine, that by rewarding of such men other might be allured
to folow their good life. As for the prayers and the divine
service, it were me[e]t the fautes were drawen out, as it
was apointed, by lerned men, and so the boke to be esta-
bliabid, and al men willed to come thereunto, to heire the
service, as I have put in remembrancis in articles touching
the statutes of this Parliement. But for discipline I wold
wish no authority geven generally to all bishops, but that
commission be geven to those that be of the best sort of them,
to exercise it in their diocesis.

This moch generally for religion.

Temporell Regiment.

The temporell regiment consisteth in well ordering, en-
riching, and defending the hole bodye politique of the commenwelth, and every parte of the hole, so one hurt not th'
other. The example whereof may be best taken of a man's
body. For even as the arme defendith, helpith, and aydeth
the hole body, chefely the head, so ought servingmen and
gentlemen chefly and such like kind of peple be alwayes
redy to defence of their countrye, and cheifly of their superiour and governour, and ought in all thinges be vigilant
and paynfull for th' encreasing and ayding of ther countrye.
And forasmouch as they in serving their king and countrey
have divers great and manyfold charges, even as the arme
doth many times beare great streassis for defence of the
heade and bodye, having no kind of way to enrich themself, neither by marchaundise, neither by handicraft, neither
by husbandrye, as the arme doth decoct no meat it self, nor
engendreth no blude, therefor even as the stomake, liver,
and lightes, wich partes engendre the bludd, doth send
nourishement to the armes and legges, sufficient to strengh-

then the part, even so must the artificers so use their gaine
in working, and so truely and justly make that that they
worke, the merchauntes must so sell there ware and so labour
to bring in straung commodites, the husbandmen must pay
such rente, and so sell thinges that come of th' encrease of
the ground, that the handis and the leggis, that is to say,
the stats of gentlemen and of servingmen may well doo the
commenwealth that service they ought to doa. And as the
gentlemen and servingmen ought to be provided for, so
ought not they neither have so much as they have in Fraunce,
where the pesauntrie is of no valew, neither yet medle in
other occupations. For the armes and leggis doth never
draw the hole bloud from the leivir, but leavith it sufficient
to worke on, neither medle in any kind of engendring of
bloud. No nor no one parte of the body doth serve for tow
occupacions. Even so neither the gentleman ought to be a
fermour, nor the merchaunt an artifisour, but to have his
arte particularly. Furthermore, no member in a wel
fashioned and hole body is to[o] bigg for the proporcion of
the body. So must their be in a wel orderid commenwealth
no person that shall have more then the proportion of the
country will beare. For as it is convenient to enrich the
country so is it hurtful immoderately to enrich any one part.
I thinke this country can beare no merchaunt to have
more land than 100 li., no husbandman or fermour worth
above 100 or 200 li., no artificer above 100 marc, no labourer
much more than he spendith. I speake now generally, and
in such cases may faile in some one particulare. But this is
sure, this comenwelth may not beare one man to have more
then 2 farmes, then one benefice, then 2,000 shepe, and one
kind of art to live by. Wherfor, as in the body no part hath
to[o] much or to[o] litle, so in a commenwelth ought
every part to have *ad victum et non ad saturitatem*. And

4

as ther is no parte admitted in the body that doth not
worke and take payne, so ought ther no part of the commenwealth to be but laborsom in his vocation. The gentleman ought to labour in service in his country, the serving-
man ought to waite diligently on his master, the artificer
ought to labour in his worke, the husbandmane in tilling
the grounde, the merchaunte in passing the tempestes, but
the vagaboundis ought clerely to be banished, as is the
superfluouse humour in the body, that is to say the spitel
and filth, wich, because it is for no use, is put out by the
strenght of nature. This is the true ordering of the state of
a well-fashioned commenwealth, that every part do obey
on[e] hed, on[e] gouvernour, on[e] law, as all partis of the
body obey the hedd, agree among themself, and on[e] not to
eat another up through gredines, but that we see that
ordre, moderation, and reason bridell th' affections. But
this is most of all to be had in a commenweale wel ordred,
that the lawes and ordinaunces be wel executed, duely
obeyed, and ministred without corruption. Now, having
seen how thinges ought to be, let us first see how now they
be ordered, and in what state they stand now, and then
goe forward to seke a remedye.

The first point in ordering the comenwealth we touched
was that the gentlemen, noblemen, and servingmen should
stand stoutly to defence of their superiour and gouvernour,
and should be painfull in ordering their country; wich thing,
although in some part and the most part be well (thankis
be to God), yet in some partis, is not absolutly, wich I
shal show hereafter particularly. But the second point,
for maintenaunce of the State and of nobles of landed men,
is ill loked to. For that state of gentlemen and noblemen
which is truly to be termid the state of noblesse hath al-
only not encreased the gaine of living. For merchauntes

have inhaunsed their ware, firmors have inhaunsed their
corne and cattell, labourers their wages, artificers the price
of their workmanship, mariners and botesmen their hire for
service, whereby they recompense the losse of thinges they
bye; but the most part of true gentlemen (I meane not
theis ferming gentlemen, nor clarking knightes) have litle or
nothing encreased their rentes; yet their housekeping is dearer
their meat is dearer, their liveries dearer, their wagis greater,
wich thing at leugth, if speedy remedy be not hadd, will
bring that stale into utter ruine (quod absit). The artificers
work falsely, the clothiers use deceit in cloth, the masons in
bilding, the clokmakers in their clokkes, the joyner in his
working of timber, and so furth al other almost, to th'
intent they wold have men cum oftener to them for amend-
ing their thinges, and so have more gaine, although at the
beginning they take out of measure. The merchauntes
aventure not to bring in straung commodites, but loyter at
home, send furth smalle hoyes with 2 or 3 mariners, occupy
exchaung of money, by and sell vitaile, steale out bullion,
corne, vitaile, wood, and such like thinges out of the realme,
and sell their ware unreasonably. The husbandmen and
fermours take their ground at a small rent, and dwell not
on it, but lett it to poore men for treible the rent they take
it for, and sell their flesh, corne, milke, butter, etc., at
unreasonable prices. The gentleman, constrayned by necessite
and poverty, becommeth a fermour, a grasier, or a shep-
master; the grasier, the fermour, the merchaunt become
landed men, and call themself gentlemen, though they be
churles. Yea, the fermour will have ten fermes, some 20,
and woll be a pedlare merchaunt; the artificer will leave the
towne, and for his more passetemps will live in the countrie;
yea, and more than that, will be a justice of peax, and will
think skorne to have it denied him, so lordly be they now

adaies. For now they are not content with 2,000 sheep, but they must have 20,000, or els they think themselfes not well ; they must 20 mile square their owne land, or full of their farmes, and 4 or 5 craftes to live by is to[o] litle, such helhoundes be they. For idle persons their were never I thinke more than be now ; the warres (men thinke) is the cause thereof, wich persons can do nothing but robb and steale. But slake execution of the lawes hath bene the chiefest sore of all. The lawes hath ben manifestly broken, the offendours punished, and either by bribery or folish pitey escaped punishment. The dissension and disagreement both for private matters, and also in matters of religion, hath bene, no litle cause, but the principall hath bene the disobedient and contentiouse talking and doyng of the folish and fond peple, wich for lake of teaching have wandred and broken, wilfully and disobediently, the lawes of this realme. The lawers also and judges have much offended in corruption and bribery. Furthermore, they doe now adays much use to forestall not only privat markettes of corne and vitaile, wherby they inhauns the price thereof, but also send to the sea to aborde shippes and take the wine, sugare, datis, or any other ware, and bring it to London, wheare they sell double the price. What shal I say of those that by and sell offices of trust, that impropriat beneficies, that destroy timber, that not considering the sustayning of men of their [corn], tourne till-ground to pasture, that use excease in apparell, in diet, and in buylding, of enclosures of wastes and commons, of those that cast fals and sediciouse billes, but that the thing is so tediouse, long, and lamentable to entreat of the particulars that I ame wery to goe any further in the particurals. Wherefore I will ceasse, having told the worst, bicause the best will save it self.

7

Nowe I will begine to entreate of a remedy. The ill in this commenwealth, as I have before said, standeth in deceitful working of artificers, using of exchaung and usury, making vent with hoyes only into Flaundres, conveying of bullion, lead, belmetall, coper, wood, iron, fishe, corne, and catell beyond sea, enhaunsing of rentes, using t[w]o artes to live by, keeping of many sheep and many farmes, idlenes of peple, disobedience of the lower sort, byijng and selling of offices, impropriating benefices, tourning till-ground to pasture, exceding in apparell, diet, and buylding, enclosing of commons, casting of ill and sedicious billes.

Thies soores must be curid with these medecins or pleastres: 1. Good education; 2. Devising of good lawes; 3. Executing the lawes justly, without respect of persons; 4. Example of rulers; 5. Punishing of vagaboundis and idel persons; 6. Encouraging the good; 7. Ordering wel the customers; 8. Engendring frendship in al the partes of the commenwealth. Thies be the chief pointes that tend to order well the bole commenwelth. And for the first, as it is in ordre first, so it seamith to be in dignitie and degree. For Horace saith very wisely, " *Quo est imbuta recens servabit odorem testa diu.*" With whatsoever thing the new vessel is imbrued it will long kepe the savour, saith Horace, meaning that for the most part men be as they be brought up, and that men kepe longest the savour of their first bringing up. Wherefore seing that it seameth so necessary a thing, we will shew our device therein. Youth must be brought up, some in husbandrye, some in working, graving, gilding, joyning, printing, making of clothes, even from their tendrest age, to th' intent they may not when they come to man's estate loyter as they doe now adays and neglect; but thinke their travell swete and honest. And for this purpose wold I wishe that artificers and other were either commaunded to bring up their sonnes in like trade, or else have some places appointed them in every good toune where they shuld be prentises, and bound to certein kind of conditions. Also that those vagaboundis that take children and teach them to begge, should according to their demerites be worthely punished.

This shal well ease and remedie the deceitful working of thinges, disobedience of the lower sort, casting of sedicious billes, and wil clerely take away the idlenes of pcple.

2. Devising of good lawes. I have shewed mine opinion heretofore what statute I think most necessary to be enacted this sessions. Nevertheles I wold wishe that beside them, hereafter, when time shal serve, the superflous and tediouse statutes were brought into one summe together, and made more plaine and short, to th' intent that men might the bettor understaund them, wich thing shal moch help to avaunce the profit of the commonweale.

3. Neverthelesse, when all thies lawes be made, established, and enacted, they serve to noe purpose, except they be fully and duely executed. Bi whom? By those that have authorite to execute. That is to say, the noblemen and the justices of pcax. Wherefore I wold wishe that after this Parliement were ended they noblemen, except a few that shold be with me, went to their countrois, and their should see the statutes fully and duely executed, and that those men shuld be put from being justices of pcax that be touched or blotted with thos vices that be against thies new laws to be established. For no man that is in faut himself can punish another for the sam offence. *Turpe est doctori cum culpa redarguit ipsum.* And thies justices being put out, their is no dout for the execution of the lawes.

www.ingramcontent.com/pod-product-compliance
Lightning Source LLC
Chambersburg PA
CBHW020540270326
41927CB00006B/663

9783741155475